# STRONGER WRITING SKILLS FOR TEENS

## Modes, Methods, and Materials That Work

**Gregory Berry**

ROWMAN & LITTLEFIELD
Lanham • Boulder • New York • London

Published by Rowman & Littlefield
An imprint of The Rowman & Littlefield Publishing Group, Inc.
4501 Forbes Boulevard, Suite 200, Lanham, Maryland 20706
www.rowman.com

Unit A, Whitacre Mews, 26-34 Stannary Street, London SE11 4AB

British Library Cataloguing in Publication Information Available

**Library of Congress Cataloging-in-Publication Data**

Name: Berry, Gregory (Gregory Wayne), author.
Title: Stronger writing skills for teens : modes, methods, and materials that work / Gregory Berry.
Description: Lanham : Rowman & Littlefield, [2018] | Includes bibliographical references and index.
Identifiers: LCCN 2018011815 (print) | LCCN 2018021362 (ebook) | ISBN 9781475841671 (ebook) | ISBN 9781475841657 (cloth : alk. paper) | ISBN 9781475841664 (pbk. : alk. paper)
Subjects: LCSH: English language—Composition and exercises—Study and teaching (Middle school) | English language—Composition and exercises—Study and teaching (Secondary) | Language arts (Middle school)—Standards—United States. | Language arts (Secondary)—Standards—United States.
Classification: LCC LB1631 (ebook) | LCC LB1631 .B42 2018 (print) | DDC 808/.0420712—dc23
LC record available at https://lccn.loc.gov/2018011815

♾ ™ The paper used in this publication meets the minimum requirements of American National Standard for Information Sciences Permanence of Paper for Printed Library Materials, ANSI/NISO Z39.48-1992.

Printed in the United States of America

# STRONGER WRITING SKILLS FOR TEENS

# Praise for *Stronger Writing Skills for Teens*

"*Stronger Writing Skills for Teens* takes the much-needed growth mind-set approach to writing—all students can become successful writers given the appropriate instruction, modeling, and practice. Berry combines his own expertise in this field with the work of esteemed colleagues to create a practical, intelligible volume for teachers to use as they facilitate students' learning and mastery of the Common Core writing standards. Reading Berry's book is akin to attending an outstanding professional development session where educators return to their classrooms with a vast array of writing strategies and tools that can, and should, be implemented immediately."—Anne DePiero, instructional mentor and AVID co-coordinator, South Salem High School

"Honest, research-driven, and thoughtfully organized, this would be a great handbook for any new English teacher to draw from when starting out in the profession. Greg Berry's *Stronger Writing Skills for Teens: Modes, Methods, and Materials That Work* provides teachers with a synthesis of researched and reliable methods for teaching writing. From front-loading vocabulary and concepts, to assessing writing, to latest trends and research, this easy-to-navigate text provides ideas and processes for those looking to refine their craft of the teaching of writing."—Kari Caulder, literacy and language arts specialist, Salem-Keizer Public Schools

# CONTENTS

# PREFACE

This book has grown out of my strong conviction of the importance of writing skills and the power of good writing instruction. This conviction is part of a more general certainty, based on more than thirty years in the teaching profession, that communication and literacy skills are the key to learning in all areas of the curriculum, a theme that has been woven into all of my recent writing. In an ever-changing and more globalized world, where workers need to have higher-level technical skills, literacy and writing skills are and will be more important than ever.

While all literacy skills are important, I am convinced that writing is one of the most fundamentally important skills students can have. It prepares them for future academic work in community colleges and universities, for their roles as citizens, and for their future careers. The earlier that teens develop strong writing skills, the more it will benefit them in their future. Research shows that some form of writing is part of almost all careers (Lannon & Gurak, 2011).

It is important to note that writing is a skill and not a talent, much like any other skill, and it can be taught and learned by all students. I frequently point out to students that writing well does not require some sort of special talent that only some people possess. While some students may have a special talent with language and writing, every student can learn to write well. Much like playing basketball or playing the piano, practice, along with coaching and guidance from teachers and others, brings improvement.

I am also quick to point out to students that, if they want to improve as writers, the best thing they can do is read—read anything and everything they can—and read a lot. Students who are good readers are generally also good writers. This is because we use the reading that we do as a model for our own writing. We learn to write by imitation, and when we read, we observe the techniques that writers use, the words that they choose, how they structure their writing, how they create a personal writing style, and how their voices come through in the writing. We unconsciously transfer these things into our own writing. As a result, our writing improves, and so does our vocabulary.

Writing, however, is also hard work. It requires effort, practice, and dedication to master. If we can help students understand the importance of writing, not only as a form of expression and a creative outlet, but also for their future lives and careers, then we can better motivate them to do the hard work necessary to learn to write well. My hope is that this book offers some suggestions and strategies for helping students develop solid writing skills.

It has been clearly established by much research that students in middle and high school need to spend more time engaging in both reading and writing in order to build solid literacy skills. In his book *Teaching Adolescent Writers*, Gallagher (2006) argues that students need to spend more time writing in schools, that teachers need to model good writing for students, and that students need to study other writers. They also need choice in their writing topics, and they need to write for authentic audiences and purposes.

While the Common Core State Standards promised that students would be required to engage in more writing to learn in all content areas, the reality is that, today, students are doing too little writing in school and are too often graduating from high school lacking the writing skills necessary for successful futures in college and the world of work.

In 2007, an Alliance for Excellent Education report warned that US students were failing in basic writing standards; that teachers were relying on the rigid and formulaic five-paragraph essay format; and that teachers were placing too much emphasis on grammar and spelling to the exclusion of content, critical thinking, analysis and interpretation, and the writing process (Graham & Perin, 2007).

An *Education Week* article notes that many students lack writing proficiency and points out that results from the 2011 National Assessment of Educational Progress (NAEP), which for the first time reflects scores on a computer-based assessment, still show only one-quarter of eighth- and twelfth-graders performed at the proficient level or higher, with black and Hispanic students scoring even lower (Fleming, 2012). Only 27 percent of students in both eighth and twelfth grades scored at or above the proficient level. Achievement gaps for different groups were also evident. At the twelfth-grade level, 9 percent of black students and 12 percent of Latino students scored proficient or higher, compared with 34 percent of white students. Also, females outperformed males at both grade levels (Fleming, 2012).

Colleges and universities often report that students are coming into college as freshmen poorly prepared for writing tasks they will face in college. A Carnegie Mellon University report in 2015 discusses some of the ways students are poorly prepared to do college-level writing and explores the reasons. Their research shows that students did not do enough writing in high school, nor did they do the types of writing they are required to do in college. Students are too infrequently asked to criticize or critique an argument, propose a solution, organize and shape their writing based on the needs of the audience, or use feedback from other readers to revise (Carnegie Mellon University, 2015).

Johnson and Sieben (2016) note that, in recent years, process approaches to writing instruction have increased, but the amount of extended writing students do is very limited, and that teachers today need to use writing to develop students' abilities to engage in creative problem solving: "Writing a paper in English is not simply about getting a good grade or passing a writing test. Rather, developing writing skills and strategies can help students expand habits of mind that connect to skills and abilities that leading twenty-first century employers look for in new hires" (pp. 80–81).

The reality is that, in secondary schools today, we need to do a better job of teaching students to write. Writing is hard work for students, so they often resist it; teaching writing is also hard work for teachers, so we may be tempted to overlook opportunities to have students engage in writing.

In *Write Like This*, Kelly Gallagher (2011) asks, "How do we get students to understand that the hard work and frustration that comes with learning how to write well is worth it? How do we get students to see the importance writing can play in their adult lives? How do we change the fact that seven out of ten students are leaving high school without adequate writing skills?" (p. 8). Gallagher's answer is that we must introduce students to "real-world discourses" and provide them with "authentic modeling" from teachers and real-world texts: "We must stand next to our students and show them how real writers write" (p. 8). His book goes on to offer lots of great strategies for modeling writing and using mentor texts.

Despite the challenges of writing and the reluctance with which some students may approach it, it is important to note that many students, once they have begun to develop and polish their skills in writing, begin to enjoy it. My seniors rebel against the multiple full-page journal entries they are required to write each week, but before long, they become very attached to their journals and look forward to the daily writing opportunities they provide. The great writer William Zinsser, in the preface to the revised version of his book *On Writing Well* (2001), notes,

> Fear of writing gets planted in American schoolchildren at an early age. . . . They are led to believe that writing is a special language owned by the English teacher, available only to the humanistic few who have "a gift for words." But writing isn't a skill that some people are born with and others aren't, like a gift for art or music. Writing is talking to someone else on paper. Anybody who can think clearly can write clearly, about any subject at all. (p. xi)

Teachers in all content areas need to provide students with lots of opportunities to engage in writing, in a variety of contexts and formats, to build their general fluency and their comfort level with writing and to teach them the skills and strategies that writers use in order to compose in a variety of modes and genres.

In this book, I present some of the strategies and approaches that have worked successfully for me and my students. While you may find that some work better than others for you, many of the strategies and materials presented here can be easily adapted and modified for various contexts and classrooms. My hope is that you find here something useful to help you meet the challenge of successfully helping your students become proficient and even excellent writers.

# ACKNOWLEDGMENTS

Sincere thanks and gratitude are extended to all those individuals who have played a role in the writing and completion of this, my third book. A loving thank-you to my family members: my wonderful parents, who have always supported my every endeavor, wholeheartedly and without reservation, from my very earliest years; my siblings, cousins, aunts, and extended family; and to all my dear friends.

My deep appreciation to Dr. Tom Koerner, vice president and publisher at Rowman & Littlefield, for providing me with the chance to complete and publish this manuscript on a topic that is so important in the field of education today. Also special thanks to Ms. Emily Tuttle, assistant editor at Rowman & Littlefield, for all her help and guidance. Because of Rowman & Littlefield, I have been blessed with the opportunity of publishing my work.

I would also like to express my gratitude to my colleagues in the Salem-Keizer School District for their friendship and support. Special thanks to my colleagues Ms. Cara Fortey for her invaluable contributions to this book, to Mr. Matthew Isom for his collaboration in some of the material included in this book, and also to Mr. Dan Mills for his assistance and technological expertise. Also, my deepest gratitude to those individuals who spent their valuable time reviewing the manuscript and for their willingness to endorse it: Dr. Jason Niedermeyer, Ms. Kari Caulder, Dr. Aaron Imig, Ms. Megan Trow Garcia, and Ms. Anne DePiero.

Finally, I would like to express my thanks to all the great writing teachers I have had throughout my long academic journey and all the wonderful teachers, writers, and authors who have served as mentors and role models to me through all of my personal and professional writing.

# INTRODUCTION

Teaching writing is hard work. It's easy enough to assign writing to students, but actually teaching students the techniques and strategies that will help them become good writers is hard. My hope is that this book can help by offering some strategies and methods for teaching various modes of writing, as well as materials and approaches to help you deal with various aspects of teaching writing.

The book is intended to be a practical and useful handbook and resource for ELA teachers at the middle and high school levels and for others who are interested in building teenagers' literacy and writing skills. It focuses on quality writing instruction, beginning with an introductory chapter that establishes a clear rationale for the importance of good writing skills and the necessity for greater focus on writing instruction in schools, as well as a discussion of the various modes of writing as defined by Common Core State Standards.

Because many schools and districts are using Common Core, the first chapter reviews the Common Core Standards' approach to writing instruction. Even if you are not bound to teaching Common Core Standards, you can still find useful resources and materials for teaching writing.

Because words and language are the tools of writers, chapter 2 focuses solely on vocabulary instruction and academic language, with specific strategies for building vocabulary. This chapter is included early in the book before any discussion of separate modes and types of writing.

Chapter 3 focuses on using writing rubrics and scoring guides, not only as tools for evaluating and grading writing, but also for instructional purposes. The chapter is also included early in the book because writing rubrics are often used to score writing in general as well as writing in specific modes. Chapter 3 offers several potential sources for good rubrics as well as instructions and suggestions to help you create your own.

The middle chapters of the book turns attention to commonly taught modes or types of writing, discussing each mode in separate chapters. While Common Core uses the terms *argument, informative/explanatory*, and *narrative* to describe the three most common types of writing, in this book I use the more general terms *argument* (referred to in some contexts as *persuasive*), *expository*, and *narrative*.

Chapters 4, 5, and 6 discuss expository/explanatory, narrative, and argument writing in turn, with suggestions and strategies for teaching each particular mode of writing, from brainstorming and prewriting through the remaining stages of the writing process. Because each mode or text type requires different strategies and methods, I discuss each mode in a separate chapter. Several specific strategy ideas, suggested materials, and ways to approach teaching the modes are included.

Chapter 7 turns the attention to research writing, including suggestions for teaching the research process, from finding and evaluating source material, to note-taking methods, organizing, drafting, and revising. Two specific research performance tasks are presented: the viewpoints essay and the I-Search paper.

Chapter 8 focuses on one very important type of writing that students are asked to do in several contexts: timed and on-demand writing. Because this type of writing is prevalent in testing situations and is often high-stakes writing, it is important for us to provide students with some strategies and practice to help them successfully complete on-demand writing tasks. This chapter is included following the chapters on separate modes of writing because timed and on-demand writing tasks can be argumentative, expository/explanatory, narrative, or some combination of modes. They may also ask students to incorporate given source material in the on-demand piece.

Finally, because in the twenty-first century, students, and people in general, are writing more frequently in digital spaces and contexts and often making use of multiple media, the final chapter focuses on how to help students learn to incorporate multimodal text into their writing. It includes ways you can use features of technology to facilitate writing instruction, from brainstorming and drafting to revision and editing. The final chapter includes suggestions for incorporating multimodal text into writing, including photographs, video, audio, hyperlinks, charts, graphs, tables, and so forth. The benefits and features of such platforms as Google Classroom and Google Drive are discussed, in addition to ways to engage in individual and collaborative writing in online spaces. Finally, the chapter includes some explanation of technology tools for editing and grading, including Turnitin, autograding programs, and digital portfolios.

# THE MODES OF WRITING AND COMMON CORE STANDARDS

In order to cultivate our students' literacy skills, we must maximize the amount of time our students spend reading and writing, as both reading and writing are interrelated language arts skills. Because good writing skills are now more important than ever, this chapter and later chapters focus on suggestions and strategies to help students master various genres of writing, including research writing.

The National Council of Teachers of English (Writing Study Group of the NCTE Executive Committee, 2004) identifies eleven guidelines about the way individuals develop writing abilities, which are useful for teachers to consider when designing writing assignments and tasks for students:

1. Everyone has the capacity to write, writing can be taught, and teachers can help students become better writers.
2. People learn to write by writing.
3. Writing is a process.
4. Writing is a tool for thinking.
5. Writing grows out of many different purposes.
6. Conventions of finished and edited texts are important to readers and therefore to writers.
7. Writing and reading are related.
8. Writing has a complex relationship to talk.

9. Literacy practices are embedded in complicated social relation-ships.
10. Composing occurs in different modalities and technologies.
11. Assessment of writing involves complex, informed, human judg-ment.

In addition, the Common Core State Standards specify several standards related to the writing task, purpose and audience, noting that students need to understand how to mix modes of writing in order to produce complex text. The standards also focus on incorporating technology and collaboration into learning to write. The ten writing standards focus on text types and purposes, production and distribution of writing, research to build and present knowledge, and range of writing.

In terms of forms or genres of writing, Common Core focuses on the three standard forms of academic writing: argument, expository (which Common Core calls informative/explanatory), and narrative (Council of Chief State School Officers & National Governors Association, 2010). Anchor standard 1 for grades 6 through 12 states that students will "[w]rite arguments to support claims in an analysis of substantive topics or texts, using valid reasoning and relevant and sufficient evidence." Standard 2 states that students will "[w]rite informative/explanatory texts to examine and convey complex ideas and information clearly and accurately through the effective selection, organization, and analysis of context." Standard 3 states that students will "[w]rite narratives to develop real or imagined experiences or events using effective technique, well-chosen details, and well-structured event sequences" (Council of Chief State School Officers & National Governors Association, 2010). Note that the standards place argument writing first, followed by informative writing, because those are the primary forms of writing used in academic contexts.

The Revised Publishers' Criteria for Common Core state that, as students move up the grade levels, they should be asked to focus less on narrative forms of writing and more on argument and explanatory writing. By high school, 40 percent of the writing students do should be argument writing (Coleman & Pimentel, 2012).

Every piece of writing we compose involves a rhetorical situation: a purpose, an audience, and a form or genre. When teaching any type of writing, encourage students to think in terms of the rhetorical situation for the piece of writing they complete. Also consider giving students a real or hypothetical audience for their piece of writing rather than just generic writing prompts that lend themselves to "writing for the teacher." Thinking about the rhetorical situation helps writers make the appropriate choices for their pieces of writing. Use simple forms of communication, such as a text message to a friend or relative, a business letter, or a resume, to illustrate the elements of the rhetorical situation.

Also, encourage students to learn and practice the stages of the writing process: prewriting (brainstorming, clustering, outlining, etc.), drafting, revising, editing, and proofreading. Too many students don't write effectively because they neglect one or more of the steps in the writing process. Many students write poorly because they don't spend enough time generating a topic and thesis and planning their paper in the prewriting stage. Students also don't typically spend much time revising, nor do they know how to go about revising their essays.

Teaching students specific strategies for revising is very important. For example, ask students to write two different versions of their introduction and then determine which one they think is the most effective. Have students read through their drafts and identify places where they need to include transitional words or phrases to better connect the parts of the essay. Or ask students to identify two or more places in their drafts where readers may have questions or where they may need to provide more information, examples, or specific details. Some additional revision strategies are presented in later chapters.

A word about the five-paragraph essay: Many teachers encourage beginning writers to learn the five-paragraph essay format. This formula includes an introductory paragraph, three body paragraphs, and a conclusion. The five-paragraph essay is a very basic writing formula that may be useful for teaching essay structure, but it is also simplistic, limiting, and not helpful in preparing students for the kinds of writing assignments they will face in college and in the real world. I recommend teaching students that every piece of writing should have an introduction, body, and conclusion and probably multiple body paragraphs, but there is certainly no rule that says an essay must be five paragraphs. The five-paragraph essay becomes a straitjacket from which students cannot escape.

In a blog post, Ray Salazar (2012) argues that the five-paragraph essay leads to bad writing and essays that are simplistic and unengaging.

He presents several reasons teachers should not use this writing formula with students: (1) If we are to successfully implement Common Core standards, the five-paragraph essay is not adequate because it promotes basic summary rather than thoughtful persuasion. (2) The theses of five-paragraph essays are neither original nor debatable. (3) The five-paragraph essay does not allow students to express their ideas in an engaging way, and the structure limits their development as writers. (4) Students need to be taught to write for specific rhetorical purposes rather than in a particular format (Salazar, 2012).

Some teachers have noted that students, even college-bound seniors, who have been taught the five-paragraph essay format have a great deal of trouble breaking away from that formula. Students often come into class convinced that an essay *must* be exactly five paragraphs—no more and no less. One student recently said, "I don't know how to write anything except a five-paragraph essay." These students' papers tend to be simplistic and overly general because the five-paragraph format traps students into a formula that constrains them from writing longer, more sophisticated, well-developed pieces of writing.

Furthermore, the five-paragraph essay does not exist in the real world. It is an artificial construct designed by well-meaning teachers. Ultimately, the number of paragraphs is not important; what is important is writing a mature, thoughtful, well-developed piece that serves its purpose, meets its audience's needs, and explores the subject in a thorough and analytical way.

Encourage your students to experiment with different formats and structures for their essays. Some types of writing tend to include numerous, shorter paragraphs—sometimes even one-sentence paragraphs. Students can also incorporate dialogue, and introductions and conclusions can often be creative as well.

Teaching writing requires teachers, especially ELA teachers, to spend a lot of time evaluating and providing feedback—grading. How we can successfully manage the paper load? Those of us who teach English are used to the stacks of papers piled up on our desks, waiting to be graded, and the stress they create.

Giving students meaningful feedback is time consuming. However, we can consider quicker and more efficient ways of providing feedback to students, including using peer-response activities; conferencing with students; and other strategies, such as having students write three essays and then deciding which one they want to submit for a grade or grading only a portion of student papers.

Also, consider making use of technology resources to facilitate the grading process. Students can do some of their writing in online formats, and you can do the grading online as well. If you have students do some of their writing online, for example in online spaces, then you can easily respond and provide feedback on the computer. You might also consider using Google Classroom and setting up classes by period number. Students can submit their writing online, and you can evaluate and provide feedback much more quickly. (See additional suggestions for technology for writing assessment in chapter 9).

## KEY IDEAS IN THIS CHAPTER

- Good writing skills are crucial, and it is imperative that we help students master various genres of writing.
- Several Common Core State Standards relate to writing task, purpose, and audience.
- All writing involves a rhetorical situation, including purpose, audience, and form or genre.
- Students need to learn to use all the stages of the writing process, including revision.
- The five-paragraph essay is a basic writing formula but is simplistic and limiting for students.
- Teaching writing requires a lot of time evaluating and providing feedback, but there are several ways to facilitate the grading process.

# 2

# VOCABULARY AND ACADEMIC LANGUAGE

Words are a writer's most important tool. We already know that vocabulary knowledge is a fundamental element of good reading comprehension and also crucial if students want to score well on such standardized tests as the ACT and SAT. In fact, as much as 80 percent of students' reading comprehension, as reflected in test scores, is based on their vocabularies (Reutzel & Cooter, 2015). But vocabulary knowledge is also crucial in terms of students' ability to write well. Students who have good vocabularies are better writers because they have a broader range of words to draw from when writing.

We also know that the traditional methods of teaching vocabulary are not very effective. Giving students a list of words and having them look up the definitions in the dictionary, memorize the definitions, and take vocabulary quizzes or tests is not an effective way for students to learn new vocabulary. This method does not help students to internalize the word meanings or make them part of their working vocabularies. The best way for everyone to learn new words is by increasing the amount of reading we do, so that we are learning new words in context and through repeated exposure to them.

Because of the importance of vocabulary, this chapter discusses vocabulary instruction in the context of writing instruction and includes discussion of academic language and domain-specific words. The Common Core State Standards for both reading and language touch on vocabulary. Students are expected to be able to determine the meanings of words and phrases as they are used in a text as well as understand words and phrases used figuratively.

The language standards for grades 9 through 12 include a section on "Vocabulary Acquisition and Use." Anchor standard 4 for grades 9 and 10 specifies that students should be able to "determine or clarify the meaning of unknown and multiple-meaning words and phrases based on grades 9–10 reading and content, choosing flexibly from a range of strategies." The subpoints include the following strategies: using context clues, using patterns of word changes to indicate different meanings and parts of speech, consulting reference materials, and verifying preliminary determination of meaning by checking the meaning in content or in a dictionary (Council of Chief State School Officers & National Governors Association, 2010). Anchor standard 5 focuses on "understanding of figurative language, word relationships, and nuances in word meaning." Finally, anchor standard 6 addresses "general academic and domain-specific words and phrases, sufficient for reading, writing, speaking, and listening at the college and career readiness level" (Council of Chief State School Officers & National Governors Association, 2010).

State scoring guides for writing often include a specific criterion for "word choice." For example, the Oregon State Official Scoring Guide, one in which each trait is scored on a six-point scale, specifies that a score of 4 is passing in word choice. Although the trait "word choice" is not one required to meet the graduation requirement, the state includes word choice as a separate trait in order to recognize its importance in good writing. The score of 4 for word choice states, "Words effectively convey the intended message. The writer employs a variety of words that are functional and appropriate to audience and purpose."

Bullets underneath the score point heading also address "functional and precise" domain-specific language; accurate academic language; technical language or jargon that is not confusing; a general avoidance of clichés; and some carefully selected metaphors, similes, and analogies. Word choice is a crucial element of writing, and a good variety of well-selected words can make the difference between an average student paper and an excellent one. In the context of our writing instruction, we must make it a point to help students improve their word choice.

So how do we help students develop an adequate and appropriate level of vocabulary in order to express what they want to say when writing? When students are expected to write in content areas other than ELA, they also need to be able to call on academic language and domain-specific words, phrases, and terminology required within the discipline. We can teach students some common academic and domain-specific vocabulary and help them understand how words can be used differently, depending on the content area.

For example, consider the word *proof* and all the separate meanings it has in different contexts. *Proof* is defined in Dictionary.com as

- evidence sufficient to establish a thing as true or to produce belief in its truth . . . anything serving as evidence
- the act of testing or making a trial of anything
- the establishment of the truth of anything, demonstration
- in judicial proceedings, evidence having probative weight
- an arithmetical operation serving to check the correctness of a calculation
- a sequence of steps, statements, or demonstrations that leads to a valid conclusion
- a test to determine the quality, durability, etc., of materials used in manufacture
- the arbitrary standard strength of an alcoholic liquor
- in photography, a trial print from a negative
- in printing, a trial impression, as of composed type, taken to correct errors and make alterations
- in printmaking, an impression taken from a plate or the like to show the quality or condition of work during the process of execution
- in numismatics, one of a limited number of coins of a new issue struck from polished dies on a blank having a polished or matte surface
- the state of having been tested and approved
- proved strength, as of armor
- in cooking, to test the effectiveness of yeast as by combining with warm water so that a bubbling action occurs

As we can see, the term *proof* is used in related but very different ways in the various fields of math, logic, science, art, journalism, photography, minting, culinary arts, manufacturing, and writing. The following are some general tips and strategies for helping students build a solid vocabulary.

Take advantage of every opportunity to teach students new words. When reading any type of text in class, literary or informational, identify words that students may be unfamiliar with. Discuss the words, their other forms, and other contexts in which they might appear. When new words come up in discussion, write them on the board and discuss their meaning with the class. The best vocabulary instruction may come from an incidental learning approach because the more the students are exposed to language through reading and listening, the more words they will learn and incorporate into their own vocabularies.

A simple Google search will provide you with a good "academic word list." You will see such words as *analyze, acquire, generate, construct, facilitate, differentiate, assess, constitute, derive,* and *distribute.* You will also be surprised how many of your students are unfamiliar with the meaning of many of these terms that are commonly used in multiple contexts and disciplines. You can make the word list available to students as well as incorporate the words into your lessons and teaching as frequently as possible.

If your students keep a class journal or spiral notebook, have them create a section for new vocabulary words they are learning as they are working on their reading and writing skills. Have students add as many words as they can each week; tell them the words can come from their reading, things they see online, words they hear in conversation, words that they encounter in the media, or by any other means. Have them write a definition of the words, but ask them to write the definition in their own words rather than copying from a dictionary. You might also ask them to write a sentence that correctly uses the words in order to practice using them. Students who are visual learners might also want to draw a sketch or picture of some kind to help them remember the meanings.

Teach students common prefixes, suffixes, and roots. Many words in our language come from Greek and Latin, so these word parts are crucial to our understanding of word meaning. When students begin to understand the meaning of certain prefixes, roots, or suffixes, they will then more easily be able to interpret words they use those same word parts. For example, consider the root word *aud*. Students will probably be able to identify such words as *audio, audible, audience*, and perhaps even *auditorium*. Doing a Google search for a word bench or list of "common prefixes, suffixes, and roots" will provide you with lots of options. You can easily print a list of Greek and Latin roots for your students, such as the one available from Glendale Community College (http://english.glendale.cc.ca.us/roots.dict.html). In the book *Literacy for Learning*, Berry (2014) provides a useful table of "Common Prefixes, Roots, and Suffixes." Focus on teaching the most common prefixes, roots, and suffixes—those that are used in a number of different words and contexts.

Find a short passage of text, literary or informational, that contains fairly simplistic language. Have students work with a partner to read through the passage to identify and highlight simple word choices, such as *happy, sad, mad, bad, good, nice, things*, or *great*. Ask them to identify as many words as they can and then use their smartphones, a dictionary, or a thesaurus to find better alternatives to the simple, general, and overused words.

Use Quizlet (www.quizlet.com) as an online tool for vocabulary study. If you use weekly vocabulary words or unit-based vocabulary, then you can easily set up classes and vocabulary study activities with flashcards in Quizlet. Students can also use Quizlet independently to create their own flashcards and vocabulary study sets. You can also choose from flashcards and study sets created by other users.

Occasionally, read a short piece of literature or nonfiction text to students, or have them read along while you read aloud. As you read, stop frequently to talk about the specific language that the writer is using, and ask students to consider why the author made the particular word choices he or she did. Also identify words that students are not likely to know. When students hear rich, strong word choices in the writing of good writers read aloud, they can better understand the power and importance of good word choice and will begin experimenting with improving their own word choice in their writing. This exercise is particularly effective with rich, descriptive passages and passages of creative writing.

Make copies of any piece of text, perhaps a well-written student essay or a passage from a short story or novel. Hand out the copies to students, and have them read the passage with a highlighter, highlighting any words that they think are powerful, effectively used, creative, striking, or puzzling or that they simply like. After the highlighting, have students share with partners or small groups, comparing which words or phrases they highlighted and explaining why they chose those particular words. They can use their smartphones or laptops to look up any words that they may not know or be able to guess the meanings of. The more students have the opportunity to read good pieces of writing and observe the techniques and language choices that writers use, the better their own writing will become.

Verbs are the words that have the greatest power in writing. Chapter 5 presents the "Vivid Verb" strategy, which is a good way to help students to improve their use of verbs. The website Writers Helping Writers (http://writershelpingwriters.net) has a very good active verbs list. Strong verbs more powerfully and creatively express the writer's message. Make a list of sentences that all have weak, simple verbs, such as *go*, *do*, *make*, *give*, *take*, and *put*; include forms of *be* verbs, like *is*, *was*, *have*, *has*, and *are*. For example, you might present these sentences to students:

1. Justin was late picking up his date.
2. I put the book carefully on the table.
3. For breakfast this morning, my mother made a soufflé.
4. When I got out of school, I went to the park to skateboard.
5. I gave my stuffed toy to my little sister.
6. Joshua is now the manager of the whole store.
7. I love to go outside on a nice, sunny day.
8. I did all my homework, even though it took me all night.
9. The coach had an argument with the referee after the call.
10. Our class had a great discussion today.
11. My family has a ten-acre farm just outside of town.
12. In history, Lincoln is the greatest president.

First, have students underline the verb in each sentence. Then, have them work with a partner to brainstorm better, stronger verbs to replace the weak verbs in these sentences. You might want to do the first couple together in order to illustrate the process for students. For example, students could rephrase number 1 as "Justin arrived late," "Justin sauntered in," "Justin appeared," or "Justin waltzed in late." If students need to rewrite the sentence a bit in order to use a stronger verb, then encourage them to do so. Have students share their final sentences with the class.

Next, have students do the same process with one of their own drafts. After students have completed a draft of a paragraph or essay, ask them to reread the paper and highlight all of the verbs. Tell them that, if they have trouble figuring out what the verb is, then you can help them. Have them refer to a list of strong verbs and consider how effective their use of verbs is throughout the paper. Ask them to use a dictionary or thesaurus if they need to and identify at least a few verbs that could be revised so they are strong, more vivid, more specific, or more powerful.

Again, using rough drafts, have students choose one paragraph or one page in their papers. Ask them to underline all of the verbs in the paragraph or page, and then consider which verbs could be replaced with more active, dynamic, or vibrant verbs. Have them focus on trying to eliminate any forms of the *be* verb. Next, have students focus on the other words in the paragraph, specifically nouns, adverbs, and adjectives. Are there any vague, general nouns that could be replaced with more specific ones? Identify places where additional adjectives could be added and where adverbs might be replaced with better ones. Have them share their revisions with a partner.

Two figures show different students' papers. Figure 2.1, Cindy's paper, demonstrates how she made several revisions in the word choice, including verbs. Notice that Cindy replaced the verbs *are* with *include*, *known* with *renowned*, and *see* with *regard*. She also made several other improvements in the word choice, such as changing *matter* to *feat* and adding other more-specific nouns and descriptive phrases. Figure 2.2 shows Joanna's paper. Joanna made several good revisions in verbs: she changed *considered* to *identified as*, *seen* to *perceived*, *live* to *reside*, *sacrificed* to *relinquished*, and *was* to *became*, as well as made other important revisions in word choice.

Teach students other strategies for revising the word choice in their papers. After students have completed rough drafts of an essay, have them read through their drafts. Ask them to highlight or place a star next to the phrase, sentence, or brief section that they think is the best part of the paper, the most interesting, or the most well-written. Ask

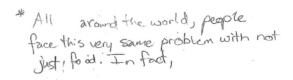

*All around the world, people face this very same problem with not just food. In fact,*

➔) Culture Drift

Culture is ~~defined~~ *defines* as a way of life and the sum of attitudes, customs, and beliefs that

distinguishes one group of people from another. For Kothari, the struggle and meandering

between just the foods of different cultures ~~is also affecting~~ *affect* her life deeply. However, even

adapting to and comprehending cuisine from different cultures is no simple ~~matter~~ *feat* for either side.

In Kothari's essay, she grappled between her family's indigenous background and her peers'

commonality. Three common differences between cultures ~~are on~~ *include* the perception of cuisine, *thesis*

values, and body language. *Could improve transition into thesis*

*repetition?*          In terms of food, based on one's birth place, a person's palate can vary ~~drastically~~ *drastically vary?*, even

from state to state in America. For example, in Oregon, we are known in other states and regions

for food that includes local fresh seafood, game meat, and wild plants, while in Texas, they are

*renowned*
~~known~~ for Southern foods that include fried foods, starches, and bitter greens. These cuisines
                                              *land, atmosphere, flora, fauna, and nurture*
have been influenced by ~~terrain, climate, flora, fauna and religion~~. Even multinational companies
                                                                      *consistently headlines a*
alter their products for each market. Take fast food. In China, KFC's ~~headline product is a~~
                    *as its mainstream product* *contain*
chicken burger, and both McDonald's and KFC ~~have~~ much more visible salad content in
       *burger. Also, both McDonald's...?*
recognition of the three food groups necessary in every meal: grains, protein and vegetables. And
                    *due to rice being a more common staple than potatoes*
rice remains more common than fries." *Add more.  Go over*

Values vary based on culture as well. Take the whaling in Japan as an example.
                    *regard*
Americans tend to ~~see~~ whales as gentile creatures, perhaps due to the influence of pop culture

**Figure 2.1.   Word choice revisions in Cindy's draft. Reprinted with permission**

each student to share the excerpt with the class, so that other students can see some of the techniques that other writers use. Ask students to also identify why they chose the passage and which word choices or techniques they used that were most effective.

When writing about specialized subjects, for example a hobby or interest, such as skateboarding, video games, or computer programming, make sure students are aware that they may be using jargon,

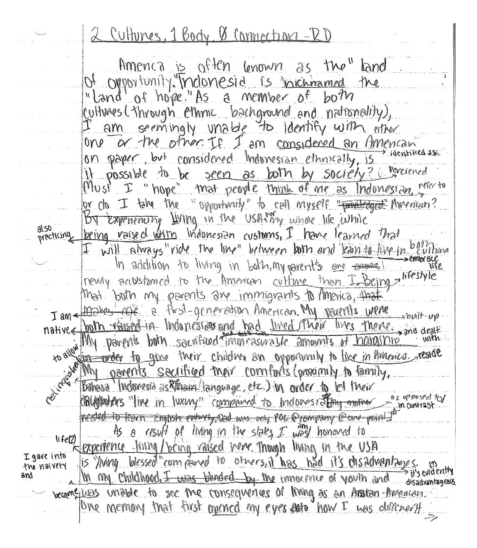

**Figure 2.2. Word choice revisions in Joanna's draft. Reprinted with permission**

specialized language, or terminology that may not be understandable for all readers. Have them go through their drafts carefully and identify any specialized terms that some readers may not know. Ask them to add in additional explanatory material or parenthetical definitions to clarify what the terms mean for an average reader.

Remind students that good writing depends on concrete, specific details and images and may also include figurative language. Ask students to locate a couple of places in their drafts where they might add in a sensory detail, a specific description, or an additional phrase or sentence that might appeal to one of the reader's senses: sight, smell, sound, taste, or touch. For example, "As I walked along the beach, the warm waves splashed against my ankles in a soothing way." Ask them to also consider adding a simile, personification, or metaphor to the paper. For example, "The stars danced in the sky as we made our way home." An alternative to this is to have students exchange papers with a partner, read each other's papers, and place a question mark next to anything that the reader would like to know more about. This helps students identify where they may need to add more specific details.

In her book *Minilessons for Revision*, Susan Geye (1997) presents a lesson plan for using imagery. Begin by writing a simple sentence on the board: "The child got mad at the teacher." Ask students whether this sentence creates a picture in the reader's mind and whether there are any details that appeal to the readers' senses. Then, show students how to write some sentences that allow the reader to see the child by using alliteration, imagery, simile, onomatopoeia, and metaphor: "Stammering a reply and stomping out the door"; "Her fist hammered the desk and she shrieked like a lioness"; "The bang of the door echoed through the hall as Billy left the room after a long detention"; "The football player—a stonebreaker on the field, a stone off of it—lamented his ineligibility" (Geye, 1997). Next, write additional sentences on the board that tell rather than show, and have students rewrite them, turning them into showing sentences that contain figurative language. For example:

- The class was boring.
- The pizza tasted great.
- The team thinks they are so cool.
- My teacher is strange.
- The mugger attacked his victim.

Ask students to share their revisions with a partner or the class, or have them choose one particular sentence, write it on a blank piece of paper, and then display them on the document camera so the entire class can see the different variations, discussing whether they are sentences that show rather than tell.

Some fun and engaging smartphone apps are available to help students build vocabulary. The apps mentioned here are free, and students can download them to their phones and spend a few minutes a couple times a week using the app. You will need to assess how many of your students do not have access to a smartphone and consider other options for them, such as use of a laptop or Chromebook. Words, Inc., is an app that provides timed rounds of play, where the player is given a word and multiple-choice options for identifying the correct meaning. Students can keep statistics and earn rankings based on amount of play. The more words that are correctly identified quickly prompts the game to provide more challenging vocabulary. Magoosh Vocabulary Builder allows students to create an account to track their progress. They then proceed through different levels of vocabulary mastery. This app also provides an option for English language learners to help them prepare for the TOEFL and IELTS. The app also reteaches words that students get wrong. The Word of the Day app teaches users a new word each day. It provides the pronunciation, definition, and two or three examples of the word being used. The user can swipe backward to see previous word of the day. Dictionary.com also has a convenient app that not only allows students to look up definitions and synonyms but also provides a word of the day sent to the phone in an alert.

Sometimes, students try too hard and go overboard in their attempt to incorporate new words and language into their papers. Remind students that most complex ideas are best when they are explained in clear and simple language, and sometimes sprinkling unusual and fancy words throughout their papers will be ineffective. If possible, find an example of a piece of writing that uses excessive, flowery, overdone language to help students understand the negative effect. Remind them that using strong verbs and specific concrete nouns are the most effective ways to revise for word choice. Also, students sometimes need to be cautioned about using slang and clichés in their writing. You can find lists of common slang words online, and warn students not to use them in school writing contexts. Remind them that academic writing uses more sophisticated language and a higher level of formality than speech, so slang terms (such as *slammin', jammin', bummed out, cool dat, dude, dawg, hyped, tight, bro, dis,* and *on fleek*), as well as idioms and clichés (like "spill the beans," "shoot the breeze," "up a creek," "dead as a doornail," and "water under the bridge"), are not appropriate or effective and should be avoided.

Organize students into groups of four when everyone has completed a rough draft. Have students rotate their papers around to every other member of the group. Each member will read the paper and serve as an editor to examine one aspect of word choice in the draft. Have each editor use a different-colored pen or pencil. One person is assigned to circle all of the abstract, general, nonspecific, or unclear nouns, such as *thing, stuff,* or *object.* Editor 2 should place a box around all the adverbs, such as *very, really,* and *extremely.* This will help students to identify if they are using too many adverbs in their paper as filler because adverbs usually don't add anything to the meaning of the sentence. Editor 3 should highlight or star any words that they don't understand. Editor 4 should underline any clichés or idioms, jargon, or overused expressions. Editor 4 examines all the verbs in the paper, offering suggestions in the margins for stronger or better verbs.

Refer to chapter 4 for some additional strategies for teaching word choice.

## KEY IDEAS IN THIS CHAPTER

- Students who have good vocabulary knowledge are generally better readers and writers.
- Common Core State Standards acknowledge the importance of vocabulary in both the reading and language standards, and state scoring guides often include a "word choice" criterion.
- When writing in content areas, students need to use academic and domain-specific words, phrases, and terms.
- Use academic word lists, apps, and other strategies to help students improve their general and academic vocabulary.
- Have students keep their own word lists for new words they encounter.
- Use excerpts from fiction and nonfiction text to analyze writers' use of language.
- Have students analyze their own use of words, including verbs and imagery, in their writing.

# 3

# USING WRITING RUBRICS AND SCORING GUIDES TO TEACH AND EVALUATE WRITING

One of our responsibilities as ELA teachers is to grade and provide feedback to our students to help them improve their writing. It would be nice if we could simply read and respond to our students' papers without the burden of having to evaluate or assign a grade. Many of us have found that writing rubrics and scoring guides are a useful way to analyze and evaluate students' writing based on specific, important criteria. Many students also find rubrics helpful because a good rubric can help them understand what they did well and what they need to work on.

## WHAT ARE RUBRICS?

Dictionary.com defines *rubric* as "any established mode of conduct or procedure, protocol," and also an "explanatory comment." *The Merriam-Webster Dictionary* defines *rubric* as a "guide listing specific criteria for grading or scoring academic papers, projects, or tests." When used for instruction and evaluation of student writing, rubrics are also much more than what these definitions encompass, and they have many more useful purposes than just scoring or grading student work.

Brookhart (2013) defines *rubric* as a "set of criteria for students' work that includes descriptions of levels of performance quality on the criteria" (p. 3) and notes that rubrics have two key elements: (1) a coherent set of criteria and (2) descriptions of the levels of performance for those criteria. They are useful tools for both teachers and students. Often the criteria for evaluation in writing rubrics include such elements as purpose, organization, detail/support, voice, and conventions. When used primarily for scoring student writing, rubrics are often referred to as "scoring guides."

It is important to clarify the difference between rubrics and checklists. For some types of assignments, checklists may be sufficient for evaluating the given assignment. Checklists, however, generally include only the criteria, with a range of scores, perhaps 1 through 5 or 1 through 10. Each criterion is then scored holistically. Checklists do not specify different levels of performance in the way that rubrics do. For this reason, rubrics are much more detailed and descriptive.

Figure 3.1 is an example checklist for an analytical report assignment in a technical writing class. You can see that a number of criteria are presented in the general categories of content, organization/arrangement, and style and page design. Each specific criterion is scored on a ten-point scale.

In contrast, Table 3.1 presents a rubric for a class presentation that includes five specific criteria and performance levels from 1 to 5. Some rubrics name or identify each specific performance level. If the levels in Table 3.1 were to be named, they might be 5 = Excellent; 4 = Strong; 3 = Good; 2 = Needs Improvement; and 1 = Poor. Many scoring guides for writing use such terms as *exceptional, strong, above average, meets the standard, does not meet the standard, proficient,* and *developing*.

Brookhart (2013) states that the key purpose of rubrics is to assess performance, whether that performance reflects a process, such as playing a musical instrument or presenting a speech, or a product, such as an essay, report, term paper, or academic project. Brookhart (2013) also argues that rubrics can be used to describe student performance rather than to judge it, which makes rubrics most useful for instructional purposes and providing feedback to students.

Although we are usually required to evaluate or assign a grade to most student writing, using a rubric to do so is preferable to just placing a holistic grade on the assignment. Some types of rubrics, those that Brookhart (2013) calls "task-specific rubrics," function as scoring guides or directions for the person scoring the work. These are the types of

**Content**

| | | | | | | | | | | |
|---|---|---|---|---|---|---|---|---|---|---|
| Report grows from clear purpose statement | 1 | 2 | 3 | 4 | 5 | 6 | 7 | 8 | 9 | 10 |
| Adequate and appropriate length | 1 | 2 | 3 | 4 | 5 | 6 | 7 | 8 | 9 | 10 |
| Limitations of analysis acknowledged | 1 | 2 | 3 | 4 | 5 | 6 | 7 | 8 | 9 | 10 |
| Visuals used to aid communication | 1 | 2 | 3 | 4 | 5 | 6 | 7 | 8 | 9 | 10 |
| Variety of sources | 1 | 2 | 3 | 4 | 5 | 6 | 7 | 8 | 9 | 10 |
| Appropriate number of sources | 1 | 2 | 3 | 4 | 5 | 6 | 7 | 8 | 9 | 10 |
| Data are unbiased | 1 | 2 | 3 | 4 | 5 | 6 | 7 | 8 | 9 | 10 |
| All data are fully interpreted | 1 | 2 | 3 | 4 | 5 | 6 | 7 | 8 | 9 | 10 |
| Documentation is adequate and consistent | 1 | 2 | 3 | 4 | 5 | 6 | 7 | 8 | 9 | 10 |
| Logical conclusions derived from interpretation | 1 | 2 | 3 | 4 | 5 | 6 | 7 | 8 | 9 | 10 |
| Recommendations appropriate to problem or question | 1 | 2 | 3 | 4 | 5 | 6 | 7 | 8 | 9 | 10 |

**Organization**

| | | | | | | | | | | |
|---|---|---|---|---|---|---|---|---|---|---|
| Distinct introduction, body, and conclusion | 1 | 2 | 3 | 4 | 5 | 6 | 7 | 8 | 9 | 10 |
| Appropriate and adequate section headings | 1 | 2 | 3 | 4 | 5 | 6 | 7 | 8 | 9 | 10 |
| Transitions between ideas or parts | 1 | 2 | 3 | 4 | 5 | 6 | 7 | 8 | 9 | 10 |
| All necessary front matter | 1 | 2 | 3 | 4 | 5 | 6 | 7 | 8 | 9 | 10 |
| All necessary end matter | 1 | 2 | 3 | 4 | 5 | 6 | 7 | 8 | 9 | 10 |

**Style and Page Design**

| | | | | | | | | | | |
|---|---|---|---|---|---|---|---|---|---|---|
| Appropriate level of technicality for audience | 1 | 2 | 3 | 4 | 5 | 6 | 7 | 8 | 9 | 10 |
| Clear, concise, fluent writing style | 1 | 2 | 3 | 4 | 5 | 6 | 7 | 8 | 9 | 10 |
| Convincing and precise use of language | 1 | 2 | 3 | 4 | 5 | 6 | 7 | 8 | 9 | 10 |
| Correct use of language and grammar | 1 | 2 | 3 | 4 | 5 | 6 | 7 | 8 | 9 | 10 |
| Correct use of conventions (spelling, capitalization, punctuation, etc.) | 1 | 2 | 3 | 4 | 5 | 6 | 7 | 8 | 9 | 10 |
| Inviting and accessible page design | 1 | 2 | 3 | 4 | 5 | 6 | 7 | 8 | 9 | 10 |
| Correct use of MLA documentation | 1 | 2 | 3 | 4 | 5 | 6 | 7 | 8 | 9 | 10 |
| Works cited format | 1 | 2 | 3 | 4 | 5 | 6 | 7 | 8 | 9 | 10 |
| Correct use of quotations, paraphrasing, summary of source material | 1 | 2 | 3 | 4 | 5 | 6 | 7 | 8 | 9 | 10 |
| Correct use of in-text citations | 1 | 2 | 3 | 4 | 5 | 6 | 7 | 8 | 9 | 10 |

**Comments:**

**Figure 3.1. Technical writing analytical report evaluation checklist**

rubrics often used in large-scale assessments and state testing. They are used to train raters of the papers in the scoring process so that raters' scores are calibrated and they are able to reach an acceptable level of reliability in scoring.

The most powerful use of rubrics, however, is not for purposes of scoring standardized and on-demand tests and performance tasks but rather to clarify for students which qualities and characteristics they should strive toward in their work. They can help students to set their

**Table 3.1.    Rubric for a class presentation**

| | *Quality of Presentation* | *Interactive* | *Handout/ Materials* | *Visual Aids* | *Accuracy* |
|---|---|---|---|---|---|
| **5** | Strong evidence of preparation, organization, and enthusiasm for topic | Presentation uses well-crafted activities, demonstration, or role-playing to actively engage and interact with all audience members | Content is presented clearly and concisely; information is well focused, accurate, relevant, highly useful, and purposeful; includes thorough bibliography | Visuals are used to make the presentation more effective; uses a variety of media | Information is highly focused, accurate, and made relevant in a meaningful way; carefully selected and pertinent information about the research behind and use of the model |
| **4** | Evidence of preparation and organization | Presentation uses demonstrations and activities which engage most audience members interactively | Content is presented clearly; information is accurate and relevant; includes bibliography | Visuals are incorporated into the presentation | Focused, accurate, and relevant info; some information about research behind and use of the model |
| **3** | Evidence of some organization and preparation; however, some elements lack preparation | Presentation includes demonstrations or role-playing, but activities do not engage audience | Some of the content is nonspecific or off topic; information is somewhat unfocused | Visuals are present and somewhat included in the presentation | Some information is nonspecific or off topic; missing application; little information regarding research behind or use of the model |
| **2** | Evidence of lack of preparation and organization | Very limited demonstrations; mostly direct instruction | Much of the content is nonspecific or off topic; handout lacks focus | Visuals are present but not referred to | Much of the content is nonspecific or off topic; presentation lacks focus |
| **1** | Little evidence of preplanning | Presentation relies solely on lecture or reading | No handouts or materials presented | Visuals are not used | Inaccurate information is presented |

own learning targets, monitor their progress, and focus on the criteria that will be assessed.

In writing instruction, rubrics can have both benefits and drawbacks, which are discussed later in this chapter. However, Brookhart (2013) observes, "Effective rubrics show students how they will know to what extent their performance passes muster on each criterion of importance, and if used formatively can also show students what their next steps should be to enhance the quality of the performance" (p. 13).

In short, rubrics can be very useful tools for writing instruction and assessment because they help define specifically what "quality work" is, for both teachers and students. Also, when students become familiar with and learn to use rubrics, they take greater responsibility for their work and may be more motivated to improve in future tasks. Another benefit is that rubrics help teachers to justify their grades or scores and more clearly explain to students why they received a particular grade. Both students and their parents generally appreciate rubrics once they have become familiar with them.

## CRITICISM OF RUBRICS

Before proceeding further, it should be noted that the use of rubrics, particularly in writing instruction and assessment, has come under fire in recent years. Critics have charged that rubrics promote standardization and formulaic writing; prevent students from taking risks; and assess students only on a given, narrow set of criteria. Alfie Kohn (2006), who has always been a harsh critic of standardized testing, argues that rubrics allow teachers to justify their grades but ultimately lead students to focus on the grade rather than the quality of their writing. He observes that they are "profoundly wrongheaded" and a "tool to promote standardization, to turn teachers into grading machines or at least allow them to pretend that what they are doing is exact and objective" (p. 12).

While Kohn does have a point, in that there are elements of writing that are highly subjective and the process of quantifying good writing is problematic, he does acknowledge that, as long as rubrics are merely one instructional tool and not used to drive instruction, they may play some beneficial role in teaching and learning. Where Kohn (2006) draws the line is when students are "given the rubric and asked to navigate by them." However, many students react to rubrics with great relief at having a clearer understanding of what is expected of them.

Mabry (1999) also argues that rubrics lead to "formulaic" writing and "simplification and homogenization" of the writing process, in essence producing "vacuous" writing. She expresses her frustration with rubrics: "Rubrics promote reliability in performance assessments by standardizing scoring, but they also standardize writing. The standardization of a skill that is fundamentally self-expressive and individualistic obstructs its assessment. And rubrics standardize the teaching of writing, which jeopardizes the learning and understanding of writing" (p. 672). Mabry goes on to argue that rubrics promote reliability in scoring but also undermine validity, thus creating a mismatch between the scoring criteria and students' actual levels of performance by causing raters to overlook other positive features of students' writing.

Rubrics typically feature anywhere from four to six criteria and usually include content, organization, and conventions. Mabry (1999) argues that the rubrics typically neglect several important aspects of writing, such as "content, logic, compelling presentation, vivid description, figurative use of language, depth of character, or significance of theme" (p. 676). While this may be true of many writing rubrics, it is not true of all.

A detailed and informative writing rubric will often address such elements as descriptive detail, language and word choice, voice, and sentence fluency. Rubrics, like any other tool, can vary greatly in quality and detail. Certainly, rubrics that are more detailed and descriptive will capture more essential elements of good writing.

While some have argued that rubrics, rather than building confident writers, prevent students from being willing to take risks, the reality is that they can be highly useful tools for guiding students, providing specific feedback, and helping students improve their work. It should be noted that Common Core State Standards have led to a return to rubrics as the approved method for evaluating student work. The testing consortiums for Common Core (SBAC and PARCC) both include rubrics written specifically for scoring writing that students do as part of the required performance tasks. Many would argue that this is not surprising because the Common Core standards themselves lead to further homogenization and standardization.

## BENEFITS OF RUBRICS

Despite the criticism and necessary concern over the use of rubrics in writing instruction, many teachers recognize the benefits of rubrics in teaching and assessing writing. While they may not always be the perfect tool, they are certainly preferable to general remarks and comments written on student papers along with a letter grade, which sometimes may seem pulled out of thin air. This type of holistic evaluation is fraught with potential bias and leaves students with feedback that is unclear and unhelpful. Rubrics can certainly be used to positively benefit classroom instruction and also to more accurately and fairly assess students' writing.

In a defense of rubrics, Spandel (2006) acknowledges that rubrics are sometimes "vaguely written, shrouded in jargon, more accusatory than helpful" and that some "emphasize a formulaic approach to writing" (p. 19). However, she argues that they can be useful for writing instruction because they are created by teachers and students who are readers and who can think carefully and reflectively about what makes good writing and how they can make their own writing better (Spandel, 2006).

As most of us know, the most important part of the writing process is revision, and if we are going to teach students to write well, then we must teach them to revise. Rubrics are a valuable tool for helping us promote thoughtful reflection about the quality of writing and guiding students in improving and revising their writing. Part of the helpfulness comes from the use of rubrics to justify teachers' reactions to student writing by showing students that our assessment is based on certain criteria (Spandel, 2006).

Spandel (2006) states, "We do need to offer reasons for our reactions to writing and to show that those reasons are based on sound criteria" (p. 21). In that sense, rubrics hold teachers accountable for the grades we assign, and they make students more understanding and accepting of those grades.

Saddler and Andrade (2004) note that good writers are able to navigate the writing process successfully and engage in self-regulation procedures, which include "goal setting, planning, self-monitoring, self-assessment, self-instruction, and self-reinforcement" (p. 48), and that good rubrics promote these characteristics. Like others, Saddler and

Andrade suggest that rubrics not only provide scaffolding for students in their journey toward becoming self-regulated writers but also that rubrics are useful for instructional purposes, especially when they are created by and with students and written in student-friendly language.

During instruction and the composing process is when rubrics are probably most useful for writers in helping them revise and edit their work. Also, rubrics can be used in the context of a peer-assessment process by serving as a tool for students to provide feedback to their peers (Saddler & Andrade, 2004). The next sections present some of the many possible instructional uses for writing rubrics.

## SOURCES FOR WRITING RUBRICS

For many of the writing assignments your students do, and for more specialized and particular types of writing, you may need to design your own rubric. However, a wide variety of writing rubrics are available online if you do not want to re-create the wheel, and many of them are very detailed and high-quality rubrics.

The Common Core Testing Consortiums use rubrics for different types of writing that are tested on the SBAC and PARCC tests. If your particular writing assignment is modeled on the types of writing required on one of these tests, and if you are providing your students practice and preparation for the test, then these rubrics are appropriate tools. The caution is, however, that these rubrics were designed for that particular type of on-demand writing task, and for general essay writing, much better writing rubrics are available.

The SBAC rubrics include one for informative and explanatory writing and one for argument writing. Both use a four-point scale and score for the following criteria: purpose/organization, evidence/elaboration, and conventions. Just by examining the criteria, one observes that many important features of good writing are not included in the rubric, including language and word choice, voice, and fluency. Sentence structure, however, is included in the conventions category.

The PARCC test updated the writing rubrics in 2014, including separate rubrics for grade 3, grades 4 and 5, and grades 6 through 11. One rubric is for the research-simulation task and literary analysis, and the other is for narrative writing. The rubrics are titled "Scoring Rubric for Prose Constructed Response Items." Like the SBAC rubrics, they use a four-point scale. Because the writing task includes reading source material, reading comprehension is also addressed in the rubric. The scoring criteria are as follows: reading comprehension of key ideas and details, writing expression, knowledge of language, and conventions.

Many states have developed their own writing rubrics, and in some cases, teachers are required to use them for scoring and preparing students for state testing. While some bias may be reflected here, the state of Oregon has for many years had one of the best six-trait writing rubrics. Prior to the era of Common Core, Oregon had its own set of standards for language arts and other content areas. Oregon writing assessment is considered one of the earliest examples of authentic writing assessment.

In Oregon, students in grades 3, 8, and 10 were required to take the state writing assessment test. Teachers and state officials in Oregon developed and over the years revised and perfected the official scoring guide for writing, which was used as the assessment tool for the state writing test. The student papers were scored by highly trained raters from around the state.

The Oregon official scoring guide for writing is known as a "six plus one" scoring guide. Papers were scored in six traits, with a seventh trait provided for writing using source material. The traits are: ideas and content, organization, voice, word choice, sentence fluency, conventions, and use of sources. Unlike many scoring guides, the Oregon scoring guide used a six-point scoring scale for each of the traits. The reason for the six-point scale is that the developers of the rubric felt strongly that they wanted the scores to allow for and reflect a wide range of performance levels in student writing rather than stopping at a proficient level. While the score of four was considered proficient and used to meet the "standard" in all traits, students who produced exceptional writing were able to earn scores of five or even six in rare cases. Student-language versions of the scoring guide were also developed. The detailed and descriptive nature of the Oregon scoring guide made it one of the most useful of writing rubrics.

When Common Core State Standards were introduced, officials in Oregon decided to revise the original Oregon scoring guide, and as of 2017–2018, the revised writing scoring guide became the official scoring guide and the standard tool to score Oregon students' writing. It is also being used to score writing work samples used to meet the Oregon essential skills graduation requirement in writing.

In the process of creating the revised scoring guide, state experts determined that the best course of action would be to create two separate revised scoring guides, one for narrative (personal or fictional) writing and one for informative/explanatory, argumentative, and research writing. The six-point scale was retained, as were all of the original scoring criteria: ideas and content, organization, voice, word choice, sentence fluency, conventions, and use of sources. While the performance levels and criteria were the same, the language was revised and changed to reflect more of the expectations, language, and terminology of Common Core. The revisions applied primarily to the traits of ideas and content, organization, voice, and word choice. The complete Oregon scoring guide is a seven-page document with one full page for each scoring trait. The original Oregon official scoring guide is now called the "Legacy Scoring Guide," and the revised scoring guides have become the new official scoring guides.

Figures 3.2, 3.3, and 3.4 include only the ideas and content page from the Oregon scoring guides. Figure 3.2 includes the ideas and content page from the original ("Legacy") Oregon scoring guide. Figure 3.3 includes the ideas and content page from the revised (now official) Oregon scoring guide for narrative writing, and Figure 3.4 includes ideas and content page from the revised (now official) scoring guide for informative/explanatory, argument, and research. By comparing the original with the revised versions, one can see how the language has been altered somewhat to reflect Common Core standards.

For purposes of scoring student papers and classroom assignments, many of us use shortened and abbreviated scoring sheets, such as the four-set scoring form page for expository writing in Figure 3.5. These pages can be printed, cut up, and stapled to student papers with the scores indicated.

In addition to state scoring guides, there are many writing rubrics available online. For older students, especially college-bound seniors, you may want to try using the ACT writing rubric. This rubric uses a six-point scoring scale, and the criteria are: ideas and analysis, development and support, organization, and language use. There is also a great rubric for general essay writing available from ReadWriteThink, called simply "Essay Rubric" (http://www.readwritethink.org/files/resources/printouts

OREGON DEPARTMENT OF EDUCATION
## OFFICIAL SCORING GUIDE, WRITING

| Ideas and Content | |
|---|---|
| **6** <br> The writing is exceptionally clear, focused, and interesting. It holds the reader's attention throughout. Main ideas stand out and are developed by strong support and rich details suitable to audience and purpose. The writing is characterized by <br> • clarity, focus, and control. <br> • main idea(s) that stand out. <br> • supporting, relevant, carefully selected details; when appropriate, use of resources provides strong, accurate, credible support. <br> • a thorough, balanced, in-depth explanation / exploration of the topic; the writing makes connections and shares insights. <br> • content and selected details that are well-suited to audience and purpose. | **5** <br> The writing is clear, focused and interesting. It holds the reader's attention. Main ideas stand out and are developed by supporting details suitable to audience and purpose. The writing is characterized by <br> • clarity, focus, and control. <br> • main idea(s) that stand out. <br> • supporting, relevant, carefully selected details; when appropriate, use of resources provides strong, accurate, credible support. <br> • a thorough, balanced explanation / exploration of the topic; the writing makes connections and shares insights. <br> • content and selected details that are well-suited to audience and purpose. |
| **4** <br> The writing is clear and focused. The reader can easily understand the main ideas. Support is present, although it may be limited or rather general. The writing is characterized by <br> • an easily identifiable purpose. <br> • clear main idea(s). <br> • supporting details that are relevant, but may be overly general or limited in places; when appropriate, resources are used to provide accurate support. <br> • a topic that is explored / explained, although developmental details may occasionally be out of balance with the main idea(s); some connections and insights may be present. <br> • content and selected details that are relevant, but perhaps not consistently well-chosen for audience and purpose. | **3** <br> The reader can understand the main ideas, although they may be overly broad or simplistic, and the results may not be effective. Supporting detail is often limited, insubstantial, overly general, or occasionally slightly off-topic. The writing is characterized by <br> • an easily identifiable purpose and main idea(s). <br> • predictable or overly-obvious main ideas; or points that echo observations heard elsewhere; or a close retelling of another work. <br> • support that is attempted, but developmental details are often limited, uneven, somewhat off-topic, predictable, or too general (e.g., a list of underdeveloped points). <br> • details that may not be well-grounded in credible resources; they may be based on clichés, stereotypes or questionable sources of information. <br> • difficulties when moving from general observations to specifics. |
| **2** <br> Main ideas and purpose are somewhat unclear or development is attempted but minimal. The writing is characterized by <br> • a purpose and main idea(s) that may require extensive inferences by the reader. <br> • minimal development; insufficient details. <br> • irrelevant details that clutter the text. <br> • extensive repetition of detail. | **1** <br> The writing lacks a central idea or purpose. The writing is characterized by <br> • ideas that are extremely limited or simply unclear. <br> • attempts at development that are minimal or nonexistent; the paper is too short to demonstrate the development of an idea. |

**Figure 3.2. Ideas and content page, Oregon "Legacy Scoring Guide." Reprinted with permission of the Oregon Department of Education**

/Essay%20Rubric.pdf). The essay rubric uses a four-point scale for the following criteria: focus and details; organization; voice; word choice; and sentence structure, grammar, mechanics, and spelling. Also, many college websites include their official writing scoring rubrics that can be

## REVISED WRITING SCORING GUIDE

### NARRATIVE WRITING (PERSONAL OR FICTIONAL NARRATIVES)

| Ideas and Content | |
|---|---|
| **6**<br>The writing is exceptionally clear, focused, and interesting. Main ideas stand out and are developed by strong support and rich details suitable to audience and purpose.<br><br>• The purpose and main idea(s) are particularly clear, focused, and controlled.<br>• Well-chosen details are significant, relevant, and carefully selected to engage and orient the audience by setting out a problem, situation, or observation.<br>• A single or multiple point(s) of view is established and a narrator and/or characters introduced.<br>• Colorful, well-developed descriptions enhance the development of setting, plot, character(s), conflict, and/or theme.<br>• The topic is thoroughly developed to present real or imagined experiences or events.<br>• Beyond telling a story, the writing makes connections and shares insights to larger issues, problems or complexities.<br>• When used, dialogue, pacing, reflection, and/or multiple plot lines enhance the experiences, events, and/or characters presented. | **5**<br>The writing is clear, focused and interesting. Main ideas stand out and are developed by supporting details suitable to audience and purpose.<br><br>• The purpose and main idea(s) are clear, focused and controlled.<br>• Supporting details are relevant and carefully selected to engage and orient the audience by setting out a problem, situation, or observation.<br>• A single or multiple point(s) of view is established and a narrator and/or characters introduced.<br>• Well-developed descriptions enhance the development of setting, plot, character(s), conflict, and/or theme.<br>• The topic is thoroughly developed to present real or imagined experiences or events.<br>• Beyond telling a story, the writing makes connections and shares insights to larger issues, problems or complexities.<br>• When used, dialogue, pacing, reflection, and/or multiple plot lines develop the experiences, events, and/or characters presented. |
| **4**<br>The writing purpose is clear and ideas are focused. The reader can easily understand the main ideas and reasoning. Support is present, generally significant, and relevant.<br><br>• The purpose is clear and main idea(s) are easily identifiable.<br>• Supporting details are typically relevant and help develop the experiences, events and/or characters.<br>• Some connections and insights may be present. | **3**<br>The reader can infer the main idea(s), although purpose and intended audience may be more difficult to discern. Details are present but non-specific, insubstantial, overly general, or occasionally slightly off-topic.<br><br>• Purpose and main idea(s) are ambiguous, predictable or overly obvious.<br>• Developmental details are often limited, uneven, somewhat off-topic, predictable, or too general.<br>• The writing may rely on clichés, or stereotypes in presenting the experiences, events and/or characters.<br>• The paper may rely on general observations rather than specifics. |
| **2**<br>Main ideas and purpose are somewhat unclear or development is vague.<br><br>• The purpose and main idea(s) may require extensive inferences by the reader.<br>• Development is indistinct and details are insufficient.<br>• Irrelevant details may clutter the text.<br>• Details may be repeated extensively | **1**<br>The writing lacks a central idea or purpose.<br><br>• Ideas are extremely limited or simply unclear.<br>• Development is missing or the paper is too short to demonstrate the development of an idea. |

**Figure 3.3.    Ideas and content page, Oregon official scoring guide for narrative writing. Reprinted with permission of the Oregon Department of Education**

accessed by students. These might be especially useful if you are trying to prepare students for college-level writing.

## REVISED WRITING SCORING GUIDE

INFORMATIVE/EXPLANATORY AND ARGUMENTATIVE WRITING AND RESEARCH PROJECTS

### Ideas and Content

| 6 | 5 |
|---|---|
| The writing is exceptionally clear, focused, and interesting. Main ideas stand out and are developed by strong support and rich details suitable to audience and purpose. | The writing is clear, focused and interesting. Main ideas stand out and are developed by supporting details suitable to audience and purpose. |
| • Main idea(s) and claims are particularly clear, focused, and controlled. | • Main idea(s) and claims are clear, focused and controlled. |
| • Details are significant, relevant, and carefully selected to accurately convey complex ideas, concepts, information, supporting claims, main ideas, and/or purpose. | • Supporting details are relevant and carefully selected to accurately convey complex ideas, concepts, information, supporting claims, main ideas, and/or purpose. |
| • When appropriate, resources provide strong, accurate, credible support. | • When appropriate, use of resources provides strong, accurate, credible support. |
| • A thorough, balanced, in-depth explanation /exploration of the topic is provided; the writing makes connections and shares insights. | • A complete, balanced explanation/exploration of the topic is provided; the writing makes connections and shares insights. |
| • Claims and counterclaims are thoroughly developed, pointing out strengths and limitations of both and anticipating audiences' knowledge, concerns, values and possible biases. | • Claims and counterclaims are well developed, pointing out strengths and limitations of both and anticipating audiences' knowledge, concerns, values and possible biases. |
| • Details are relevant and establish the substantive main idea(s) or claim(s) by using significant facts, extended definitions, concrete details, quotations or other information/evidence appropriate to audience and purpose. | • Details are relevant and establish the importance of the main idea(s) or claim(s) by using significant facts, concrete details, quotations or other information/evidence appropriate to audience and purpose. |

| 4 | 3 |
|---|---|
| The writing purpose is clear and ideas are focused. The reader can easily understand the main ideas and reasoning. Support is present, generally significant, and relevant. | The reader can infer the main idea(s), although purpose and intended audience may be more difficult to discern. Details are present but non-specific, insubstantial, overly general, or occasionally slightly off-topic. |
| • There is an easily identifiable purpose; main idea(s) /claims are clear; counterclaims are acknowledged and addressed. | • Purpose and main idea(s) are ambiguous, predictable or overly obvious. |
| • Supporting details are typically relevant and anticipate major knowledge, concerns, values and possible biases of intended audience. | • Support is offered, but developmental details are often limited, uneven, somewhat off-topic, predictable, or too general (e.g., a list of underdeveloped points). |
| • When appropriate, resources are used to provide accurate support for claims, main ideas, and/or purpose. | • Details may not reflect well-grounded, credible resources; they may be based on clichés, stereotypes or questionable sources of information. |
| • The claim or topic is explored /explained, with developmental details in balance with the main idea(s); some connections and insights may be present. | • In argumentative writing, counterclaims are ignored, ineffectively addressed, or misinterpreted. |
| • Details are generally relevant and specific, using facts, quotations or other information/evidence appropriate to audience and purpose. | • The paper may rely on general observations rather than specifics. |

| 2 | 1 |
|---|---|
| Main ideas and purpose are somewhat unclear or development is vague. | The writing lacks a central idea or purpose. |
| • The purpose and main idea(s) may require extensive inferences by the reader. | • Ideas are extremely limited or simply unclear. |
| • Development is indistinct and details are insufficient. | • Development is missing or the paper is too short to demonstrate the development of an idea. |
| • Irrelevant details may clutter the text. | |
| • Details may be repeated extensively. | |

**Figure 3.4. Ideas and content page, Oregon official scoring guide for informative/explanatory, argument, and research writing. Reprinted with permission of the Oregon Department of Education**

Another great source of rubrics is Turnitin (www.turnitin.com). If your district subscribes to this service, which provides plagiarism checking, an online grading program, and peer-editing features, then you can

**WRITING EVALUATION EXPOSITORY**

**Ideas/Content**                                          1  2  3  4  5  6
*Writing purpose is clear and ideas are focused. Reader can easily understand main ideas and reasoning. Support is present, generally significant, and relevant.*

**Organization**                                          1  2  3  4  5  6
*Organization is clear and coherent. Order and structure are present, but may seem formulaic or somewhat predictable.*

**Voice**                                                 1  2  3  4  5  6
*Writer seems committed to topic, and there may be a sense of "writing to be read." In places, writing is expressive, engaging, or sincere and establishes formal style, objective tone appropriate to audience, purpose and topic.*

**Word Choice**                                           1  2  3  4  5  6
*Words effectively convey intended message. Writer employs a variety of functional words appropriate to audience and purpose.*

**Sentence Fluency**                                      1  2  3  4  5  6
*Writing flows with mostly fluid connections between phrases or sentences. Sentence patterns are somewhat varied, contributing to ease in oral reading.*

**Conventions**                                           1  2  3  4  5  6
*Writing demonstrates control of standard writing conventions (e.g., punctuation, spelling, capitalization, grammar and usage). Errors are infrequent and minor; errors do not impede readability and meaning.*

                                                        Met   Not Met

**WRITING EVALUATION EXPOSITORY**

**Ideas/Content**                                          1  2  3  4  5  6
*Writing purpose is clear and ideas are focused. Reader can easily understand main ideas and reasoning. Support is present, generally significant, and relevant.*

**Organization**                                          1  2  3  4  5  6
*Organization is clear and coherent. Order and structure are present, but may seem formulaic or somewhat predictable.*

**Voice**                                                 1  2  3  4  5  6
*Writer seems committed to topic, and there may be a sense of "writing to be read." In places, writing is expressive, engaging, or sincere and establishes formal style, objective tone appropriate to audience, purpose and topic.*

**Word Choice**                                           1  2  3  4  5  6
*Words effectively convey intended message. Writer employs a variety of functional words appropriate to audience and purpose.*

**Sentence Fluency**                                      1  2  3  4  5  6
*Writing flows with mostly fluid connections between phrases or sentences. Sentence patterns are somewhat varied, contributing to ease in oral reading.*

**Conventions**                                           1  2  3  4  5  6
*Writing demonstrates control of standard writing conventions (e.g., punctuation, spelling, capitalization, grammar and usage). Errors are infrequent and minor; errors do not impede readability and meaning.*

                                                        Met   Not Met

**WRITING EVALUATION EXPOSITORY**

**Ideas/Content**                                          1  2  3  4  5  6
*Writing purpose is clear and ideas are focused. Reader can easily understand main ideas and reasoning. Support is present, generally significant, and relevant.*

**Organization**                                          1  2  3  4  5  6
*Organization is clear and coherent. Order and structure are present, but may seem formulaic or somewhat predictable.*

**Voice**                                                 1  2  3  4  5  6
*Writer seems committed to topic, and there may be a sense of "writing to be read." In places, writing is expressive, engaging, or sincere and establishes formal style, objective tone appropriate to audience, purpose and topic.*

**Word Choice**                                           1  2  3  4  5  6
*Words effectively convey intended message. Writer employs a variety of functional words appropriate to audience and purpose.*

**Sentence Fluency**                                      1  2  3  4  5  6
*Writing flows with mostly fluid connections between phrases or sentences. Sentence patterns are somewhat varied, contributing to ease in oral reading.*

**Conventions**                                           1  2  3  4  5  6
*Writing demonstrates control of standard writing conventions (e.g., punctuation, spelling, capitalization, grammar and usage). Errors are infrequent and minor; errors do not impede readability and meaning.*

                                                        Met   Not Met

**WRITING EVALUATION EXPOSITORY**

**Ideas/Content**                                          1  2  3  4  5  6
*Writing purpose is clear and ideas are focused. Reader can easily understand main ideas and reasoning. Support is present, generally significant, and relevant.*

**Organization**                                          1  2  3  4  5  6
*Organization is clear and coherent. Order and structure are present, but may seem formulaic or somewhat predictable.*

**Voice**                                                 1  2  3  4  5  6
*Writer seems committed to topic, and there may be a sense of "writing to be read." In places, writing is expressive, engaging, or sincere and establishes formal style, objective tone appropriate to audience, purpose and topic.*

**Word Choice**                                           1  2  3  4  5  6
*Words effectively convey intended message. Writer employs a variety of functional words appropriate to audience and purpose.*

**Sentence Fluency**                                      1  2  3  4  5  6
*Writing flows with mostly fluid connections between phrases or sentences. Sentence patterns are somewhat varied, contributing to ease in oral reading.*

**Conventions**                                           1  2  3  4  5  6
*Writing demonstrates control of standard writing conventions (e.g., punctuation, spelling, capitalization, grammar and usage). Errors are infrequent and minor; errors do not impede readability and meaning.*

                                                        Met   Not Met

**Figure 3.5.   Abbreviated four-set Oregon scoring guide for writing**

also access a variety of rubrics. Turnitin includes a bank of existing rubrics for different types of writing and also allows you to create your own rubric for assignments you can have students submit to the site. After you have logged into your account and created your classes and assignments, you can go to the "Libraries" tab and click on "Rubric/Form Manager." Once you have established settings for a given assignment in Turnitin, you can click the link to find a rubric appropriate for the assignment. The existing rubrics include those designed to reflect CCSS skills for grades 9 and 10 and grades 11 and 12. Other rubrics in the bank include those for public speaking, persuasive papers, theme analyses, general writing, research papers, commentaries, reflection papers, six-trait rubrics, paragraph writing, analytical essays, and several subject-area International Baccalaureate (IB) rubrics (see further discussion of Turnitin in chapter 9).

## CREATING YOUR OWN RUBRICS

For many assignments, especially specific types of writing assignments, modes, and styles of writing, you may want to develop your own writing rubric. Follow this general procedure:

1. Begin by identifying and listing the criteria that will be used to assess the writing. Ask yourself, "What do I want students to learn and be able to demonstrate in their writing?" The criteria should be directly related to the standards or learning outcomes. Make sure the criteria focus on elements of content rather than appearance or neatness. For example, many writing rubrics include the following criteria: purpose/focus/content, organization, sentence structure/fluency, voice, language/word choice, and conventions. If the particular assignment has other criteria that are essential to the task, then make sure they are included as well.

2. Determine your performance levels for the criteria. You can use as many levels as you wish. Most rubrics include three to six performance levels. If you use only three levels, they may be labeled "below average," "average," and "above average" or "does not meet the standard," "meets the standard," and "exceeds the standard." If you use five levels, they might be "weak," "needs improvement," "average," "above average," "excellent." Use whichever labels you feel are most appropriate for your students and the task. Try to avoid using labels that are overly negative, such as "poor quality" or "deficient."

3. Next, place the scoring criteria in columns across the top of the page. Place the performance levels from high to low down the left-hand side of the page. This creates a grid so that each level of performance can be described for each criterion. It is probably easiest to start with the middle level, the level that reflects meeting the basic standard. Determine the minimum performance that students must demonstrate to score at each particular level for each criterion. Then move up to the higher levels and then down to the lower levels.

4. Begin using the rubric to evaluate students' papers. After you have been scoring with the rubric for a while, you will begin to notice weaknesses in the rubric. You may notice that certain descriptive information has been left out of the rubric. Take note of these missing elements, and before using the rubric again, revise it. Continue revising occasionally as necessary.

As mentioned earlier in the chapter, there are many advantages to having students participate in the rubric-development process. Participating in creating the rubric allows students to think carefully about what makes good writing and what aspects and elements of their writing they should be accountable for. Gallagher (2006) describes the process he uses for creating writing rubrics with his students. He begins by handing out a blank "Essay Scoring Rubric." The rubric has five tiers for scoring criteria, and the first is reserved for assessing organization. In the process of developing each tier of the rubric, Gallagher shows students examples of pieces of writing, those that meet the standard and those that exceed. Students then discuss the characteristics and qualities they see in the writing, identify what distinguishes the proficient from the outstanding, and write comments on a blank rubric for the whole class to see. Gallagher's second tier of the writing rubric is reserved for content, and the third tier is reserved for issues of craft. The remaining two tiers are personalized for students based on the instructor's comments written on their papers. By examining models of writing for each tier, the descriptive detail of the rubric beings to take shape.

Gallagher's process is unique in that the rubric that is created and developed by students has some common assessment traits as well as some that are personalized for each student: "This means that each writer will have a rubric that will contain common elements (the first three tiers) as well as elements that are specific to each writer's needs. I ask the students to look in their papers and find the two comments I have written in the margins of their papers. Each student writes the two comments on his or her rubric" (Gallagher, 2006, pp. 161–62). Try this process or a similar process for developing a general rubric for essay writing with your students.

## INSTRUCTIONAL USES FOR RUBRICS

This final section of the chapter includes some ways that you can use writing rubrics for instructional and formative purposes. There are some suggestions for helping your students to become familiar with and comfortable using rubrics.

After students have been given a particular writing assignment, engage them in an activity to help them understand the rubric. Arrange students into groups of four, and give each group a copy of the rubric. Have the students review and discuss the rubric as a group and identify the major elements they will need to have and the things they will need to do in order to do well in the particular writing task. Ask them to write up a brief summary of their discussion to present to the class.

Place students in small groups of three to five students. Assign each group to one particular trait on the rubric. Have them study that particular trait, analyzing the language used on the scoring guide. Ask them to look up some additional information about that aspect of writing from other sources in order to learn more about what it means. For example, what elements of writing does the term *organization* refer to? Have each group create a poster to teach others about that particular writing trait. Their poster should include a definition of the trait, some instructional materials or steps for creating that element in a piece of writing, some visual elements, and one or more samples of writing that demonstrate that particular trait (e.g., good word choice or sentence fluency). Once students have finished their posters, organize a gallery walk so that students can move around the room and study the different posters created by other groups.

Involve students in creating their own rubrics, even for short writing tasks. You might try using Gallagher's method of having students examine samples of writing to identify criteria and descriptors to include on a rubric. Have each student create his or her own personal writing rubric. First have them review their portfolio or recent writing assignments and create a list of common mistakes, problems, and weaknesses in their writing. Then ask them to create their own writing rubric with at least five traits or criteria specifically addressing their writing weaknesses. If you use a peer-review or -response process with student drafts, then students can hand their personal rubric to their partner and ask him or her to use it to score the paper.

Teach students to use the writing rubric to score sample papers. Locate or collect a number of sample papers for a given assignment or a particular mode of writing. Student papers and essays from previous years work well. Give each student a copy of the writing rubric and a highlighter. Go through each trait and scoring point with students, and have them highlight the key points on the rubric in preparation for using the highlighted rubric to score sample papers. It helps if you have created a key of actual scores for all the sample papers ahead of time. Copy or display sample papers, and ask students to read and score them using the scoring guide. Remind them that each trait reflects a different aspect of writing, so some papers may have high scores in some areas and low scores in others. Tell them to avoid making immediate judgments about the papers and instead use the language of the scoring guide to determine the accurate score for each trait. After students have read and scored each paper, have a discussion with the class, surveying them to find out which score students gave the papers in each trait. Then present them with the actual scores. After students have gone through this process with a number of papers, they will calibrate their scoring to the standards and will eventually become remarkably accurate in their scoring.

Teach students to use the writing rubric to score their own papers. During the revision process, make sure students have a copy of the rubric. Ask them to carefully reread their papers and determine how they will score based on the language of the rubric. If possible, conduct quick conferences with students after they have identified which scores reflect the current quality of their writing. You might be able to offer some suggestions for what they can do to revise. Then have students write down three things they need to work on to improve the scores on their papers.

Have students work with small groups to complete a peer-review process. Give each student a copy of the rubric. Have them use a score-marking sheet with a place for making comments that they can attach to each paper they read. Have students rotate their papers around to each member of the group in turn. Ideally, each student will read every other student's paper and provide scores and commentary. Students need some guidance and direction in using the peer-review process productively. Tell them that, in their comments for other writers, they need to focus on the strengths of the paper as well as suggestions for improvement when they revise. Remind them to be constructive and supportive of other students and not to make harshly critical comments. Also teach them to use the language from the scoring guide in their written comments. For example: "You need to add some effective transitional devices between the paragraphs of your paper."

In your professional learning community (PLC) group, collect writing samples from each teacher on a common prompt, and have PLC members score the papers using the agreed-upon rubric. Compare and discuss your scoring. Try to pin down scores for each trait based on the language of the scoring guide, and calibrate the scoring of members of your group. This ensures that all teachers are scoring a given assignment accurately and fairly across classes and teachers.

Have students write a reflection based on their experiences with using the scoring guide for any of the activities mentioned here or others that you may use. Ask them to explain what was and was not effective and useful for them.

## KEY IDEAS IN THIS CHAPTER

- Writing rubrics and scoring guides are a useful tool for analyzing and evaluating students' writing.
- Rubrics have a set of criteria and descriptors of performance levels for each.
- Checklists include only a set of criteria with a range of scores.
- Rubrics can clarify for students the qualities and characteristics they should strive for in their writing.
- Rubrics have both benefits and drawbacks.

- Rubrics normally address content, organization, and conventions but may also address word choice and language. Available rubrics vary greatly in quality and level of detail.
- Rubrics can be used for instructional purposes and can provide scaffolding for students.
- There are many sources of good writing rubrics, including state writing rubrics, such as the Oregon scoring guide for writing.
- Teachers can create their own rubrics by identifying criteria and performance levels and writing a description for each performance level.
- Writing rubrics can be used for instructional and formative purposes.
- A number of strategies can be used to help students effectively use writing rubrics to evaluate their own and other students' writing.

# 4

# EXPOSITORY/EXPLANATORY WRITING

The more traditional term for writing that explains is *expository writing*. Note that Common Core chooses to call this mode of writing *informative/explanatory* rather than *expository*. Common Core writing standard 2 deals with informative and explanatory texts, and the standard itself has several subpoints. The following is writing standard 2 for grades 9 and 10, with its several supporting goals:

> Write informative/explanatory texts to examine and convey complex ideas, concepts, and information clearly and accurately through the effective selection, organization and analysis of content.

> a. Introduce a topic, organize complex ideas, concepts and information to make important connections and distinctions, include formatting (e.g., headings), graphics (e.g., figures and tables), and multimedia when useful to aiding comprehension.
> b. Develop the topic with well-chosen, relevant and sufficient facts, extended definitions, concrete details, quotations, or other information and examples appropriate to the audience's knowledge of the topic.
> c. Use appropriate and varied transitions to link the major sections of the text, create cohesion, and clarify the relationships among complex ideas and concepts.
> d. Use precise language and domain-specific vocabulary to manage the complexity of the topic.

e. Establish and maintain a formal style and objective tone while attending to the norms and conventions of the discipline in which they are writing.

f. Provide a concluding statement or section that follows from and supports the information or explanation presented (e.g., articulating implications or the significance of the topic). (Council of Chief State School Officers and National Governors Association, 2010)

You may notice that the standard for informative writing is intentionally cross-disciplinary because the most common form of writing used in multiple content areas is expository.

Expository writing is a type of writing that explains, informs, provides information, or describes something. Expository writing usually requires students to explore an idea; locate and use appropriate evidence, details, or examples; and present the information in a clear manner and appropriate form for the audience and context.

*Expository writing* is actually a general term that encompasses several different thinking processes and patterns used in a variety of academic disciplines, often used in combination with other modes. Several different modes fall under the general category of expository or informational, and students usually need direct instruction in each type in order to master them.

**Description:** Description writing is used to demonstrate students' knowledge and understanding of a topic by identifying its characteristics and features. It often provides a great deal of descriptive and sensory detail to show how an object, person, or place looks, feels, tastes, smells, and sounds. Descriptive writing is often used as one means of development for another type of essay, such as narrative or argument. Description writing can be objective and factual or subjective and personal, depending on the topic, context, and audience. Description essays generally need to include a "dominant impression," the overall idea or point you want readers to understand after reading the essay. For example, students were asked to select a specific location, space, object, or area to write a detailed description of. Javier decided to write a description of the Japanese garden at the nearby park, and his dominant impression was that the garden was a serene place of solitude and beauty where one could find peace and tranquility.

**Exemplification:** Exemplification writing illustrates a point with examples. While examples are always important in developing any type of essay, an exemplification essay is one that is developed entirely with examples. Facts, details, anecdotes, opinions, and observations are all types of material that can be used as examples to illustrate a point or thesis. Examples should be interesting, but they should also be persuasive, relevant, representative, and help explain something that might otherwise be difficult for the reader to understand. In some cases, an exemplification essay can use a single extended example. For example, if a student was writing a paper about how styles of dress reflect individual personalities, then she would want to develop the essay with specific modern fashions and examples of real or hypothetical people and their clothing choices to illustrate the point.

**Process:** Process writing occurs in a number of contexts and multiple content areas. It presents the steps or stages in a process. It is a highly sequential type of writing that depends on chronological presentation of the details. For example, recipes, directions for operating a piece of machinery, a description of a natural process or phenomenon, and procedures are all types of process writing. Process writing is a very common type of technical writing, although such pieces can also be more creative and literary.

**Definition:** Definition writing can include very brief sentence definition used in the context of a larger piece of writing or a much longer, detailed definition. This type of writing is sometimes called an *expanded definition*. Definition essays explore the meaning of a particular term or concept, usually something abstract or conceptual. They may also involve personal interpretations of the term or concept. The definition paper must use a variety of techniques, including examples, facts, details, comparison, analysis of parts, or definition by negation to clarify for the reader what the concept means. For example, students might write a definition essay for any of the following terms: capital punishment, courage, heroism, intelligence, family, devotion, or democracy.

**Comparison-contrast:** Comparison-contrast writing involves explaining and showing the reader how two or more items or topics are alike and how they are different; in other words, exploring their similarities and differences. We consider comparison-contrast as a single mode of writing because we usually do both comparing and contrasting at the same time. For example, in history, students are often asked to compare two historical figures, two periods of time, two leaders, two wars, two movements, or two forms of governments. Students might also choose to compare two types of vehicles or computers or two video games or movies. Comparison-contrast is widely used in both academic contexts and daily life.

**Cause-effect:** Cause-effect writing focuses on the relationship between two or more events. An essay can address primarily causes, primarily effects, or both at the same time. Because humans are always asking, "Why?" cause-effect writing is a powerful and important form of thinking. In academic contexts, this type of writing is sometimes called *causal analysis*. Cause-effect writing uncovers the connections between events and involves a great deal of thinking skill and analysis, especially because it is very difficult to scientifically establish a cause-and-effect relationship. For example, a student might be asked to research the topic of deforestation or acid rain and write a cause-effect essay or write an essay about the causes of student apathy. Or he might be asked to write about the effects of Prohibition in the 1920s and beyond.

**Problem-solution:** Problem-solution writing is sometimes called *problem-cause-solution* because it starts with exploring the nature of a particular problem. Generally, in order to come up with a solution to the problem, we need to identify the causes of the problem. This mode of writing may also result in a proposal for solving the problem at the end of the essay. For example, a student may choose to write about the problem of climate change, first focusing on exploring the nature and extent of the problem itself, then discussing some of the causes of the problem, and finally making some recommendations for what can be done to solve the problem or at least mitigate the effects.

**Division-classification:** Division-classification writing involves organizing a set of items. It helps us to make sense of a complex world by imposing a logical structure on it. Division and classification, much like comparison and contrast, are actually separate processes. Whereas division involves dividing something into separate parts, classification involves organizing a number of items together into categories by type or kind. For example, one could classify different types of vegetables into categories based on a number of different criteria. A student might be asked to explore and classify different types of teachers, high school courses, clubs, or electives offered. Students might also write an essay to divide and classify video games, types of popular music, or television shows.

There are also other modes of writing that are more discipline specific and that would also fall under the general heading of expository or informational writing. In English classes, students are often asked to write literary analyses, a type of analytical essay about a specific piece of literature. This type of writing presents students with a topic related to some literary element or aspect of the text (theme, conflict, character, or style). In some cases, students may choose their own topics of analysis. They should develop the paper using specific examples and quotations from the text and accurately analyze the content and themes of the text.

The following paragraphs offer some general recommendations for teaching expository writing.

First, make sure that students write a clear thesis statement for their essays. If students have been asked to address a specific prompt (such as in an essay exam), then they should make sure that their thesis statements clearly address the prompt. Check their thesis statements, and offer suggestions if the statements are too general, too specific, too broad, or not clear. Have students rewrite their thesis statements if necessary.

Many types of expository writing require students to do some research. This means that you may want to include some minilessons on research methods. Demonstrate for students how to do online searches and database searches, evaluate sources, and use research resources available in the school library.

Also guide students in the process of note taking, teaching them the difference between summary, paraphrase, and quotation. Be sure to include some discussion of plagiarism and how to cite sources according to a particular citation format (MLA or APA, for example). Teach students how to use citation makers, such as those available on research databases and other online sources, like EasyBib (www.easybib.com).

Also, consider asking students to find visuals that they can add into their papers. Many types of expository writing can be enhanced with visual material, such as photographs, maps, charts, tables, graphs, and diagrams. Students can create their own visuals or borrow them from sources, making sure to correctly cite the source of the original. Make sure students understand that they should also introduce and explain visuals in the text of their papers, not just randomly insert them into the papers. (See chapter 9 for suggestions on incorporating multimodal text.)

Provide students with a good list of transitions. During the drafting process, require them to have the list of transitions in front of them while they are writing. Have them underline or highlight their transitions so that you can check them and offer some suggestions when you review their rough drafts. The following is a good list of transitions.

———⊱〰⊰———

### Common Transitional Words and Phrases

For comparison: similarly, likewise, in the same way, besides, next

For contrast: however, on the other hand, nevertheless, in contrast, yet, on the contrary, nonetheless, but, conversely, even though, despite

For repetition/elaboration: again, next, moreover, to demonstrate, also, furthermore, another, one more, second, third

For cause and effect: because, for this reason, since, on account of, so, as a result, therefore, consequently, thus, hence

To illustrate: for example, for illustration, another example, for instance, specifically

To show time order: earlier, first, next, later, afterward, at the same time, while, during, now, simultaneously, immediately, soon, subsequently, concurrently

To show space: adjacent to, beyond, farther on, nearby, opposite of/to, here, there

To summarize/conclude: as a result, as I have stated, to repeat, to conclude, therefore, in summary, in short, as we have seen, to summarize, in sum, finally

———⊱〰⊰———

Use some sort of peer-review process, such as peer-response groups. This allows students to get some feedback from their peers about the content and organization of their papers. It also provides the additional benefit of students learning from the techniques they observe other students using in their papers. Use the checklist later in this chapter or some other simple set of questions that students respond to as they are reviewing other students' drafts.

Perhaps the hardest aspect of teaching writing, regardless of the mode, is getting students to effectively engage in revision. Most students want to write out a quick draft of the paper; get it finished as quickly as possible; and resist going back to reread, think about the effectiveness of their writing, or make changes. Students who are struggling writers may know that perhaps their drafts are not very good, but they probably won't know what to do to make them better.

There are numerous effective ways we can help students revise their writing. First, require students to bring to class a rough draft of their paper; assign a due date for it; and give points, credit, or a grade for having a completed rough draft. It is only when students actually have a rough draft in front of them that you can help provide them with specific revision techniques.

Have students work with a partner or in a small group and read their papers aloud to each other in turn. All writers typically notice many problems with their writing, including syntax problems, awkward wording, inappropriate word choices, and convention errors when reading aloud that they tend to overlook when reading their papers silently.

Teach students the concept of coherence and its importance in writing. Students must understand that all the ideas and sentences in a paragraph or paper must cohere, or hold together. This requires good organizational structure but also effective use of transitions and other words and phrases that connect ideas together. Take some sample paragraphs from student papers, from a writing textbook, or from other sample essays, and remove all the transitional words and phrases. Have your students practice revising the essays by adding in transitions of their own to connect the ideas and sentences in the paragraph and provide an organizational structure.

Next, have students evaluate the coherence in their own drafts. Give them a colored pencil, and have them read through the paper and highlight all the connecting words and transitions. This exercise will help them identify whether they have used effective and adequate transitions.

We also need to teach students about the concept of unity in writing. Good writing sticks to the topic, and all of the ideas and sentences relate to the main idea. Have students practice this concept by examining pieces of writing that are not well unified. Take some sample paragraphs from student papers, from a writing textbook, or from other sample essays, and add in a few random, irrelevant, and unrelated sentences. Then have students practice identifying the irrelevant sentences in the paragraphs. Next, ask them to reread their own essays, looking for spots where the unity might be broken.

Keep in mind that allowing students to type their papers on laptops or in the computer lab will facilitate the process of revision. Word-processing allows students to easily make changes in their texts, add additional material, delete unnecessary material, and rearrange sections of their papers. Ask students to read carefully through their drafts while working on the computer and find two or three places where they need to add some additional explanation, clarification of a point, or a specific example or detail.

Provide students with hard copies of poorly written paragraphs and short essays. Ask them to read through and mark errors, as well as note any necessary revisions, such as correcting awkward wording, rewriting unclear sentences, and so forth. Try taking sample essays and rewriting them to add in many word-choice problems, awkward sentences, unclear expressions, sentence-structure errors, and other types of convention errors to provide students with practice in revising and editing. Assign students to revise and rewrite the sample papers. Once they have done enough of this practice revising, they will be more likely to use the same process with their own drafts.

Teach students that the most important part of the writing process is revision. *Revision* means, literally, "to see again." As mentioned earlier, most students want to write one draft of their papers and then consider them finished. Unless we teach them some tools for going back and "reseeing" their writing and teach them how to revise and make changes and improvements, then it is unlikely that their writing will get better. The following are some suggestions for encouraging students to revise.

Have students write a first draft of the paper and then turn it in to you. Wait several days before you return the draft to students and ask them to revise. When we come back to a draft later, we often are able to view it with a different perspective and may be more likely to notice problems it may have. As mentioned in the previous point, there are many advantages to having students work with a typed draft, but it is also important for them to get in the habit of looking at their own handwriting on paper and making changes and revisions in the margins of their papers.

Have students reread their papers, imagining that someone else is reading it. Have them jot down a few questions they would like to ask someone reading their papers, questions that might provide some specific feedback for them on the content and organization of their writing. For example, are there any other examples I could include in paragraph 2? Is the introduction interesting? Did you notice any parts that were unclear? Next, match students up with a partner, and have them read their papers aloud to their partners and then ask their partners the questions they prepared. The partner should respond to the questions as clearly and honestly as possible, while the writer of the paper takes notes on the suggestions they offer. Partners will then switch roles. You might want to have a couple of capable students model this process for the rest of the class when asking students to do it for the first time.

Students often work harder and write better when they know that someone else besides the teacher will be reading their papers. Whenever possible, try to identify authentic audiences for students' writing. Have students write editorials to be sent to the local newspaper. Try having students write letters to a particular author whose work they have read and actually send them to the author. Consider having students write and submit their papers to online forums. Identify a target audience or audiences in the community. Or have students write an argument on a school-related issue or problem to send to the school administration or local school board. Students can also write letters to local, state, and national representatives.

Have students spend some time focusing on their introductions. Point out that the introduction should catch the reader's attention, give some background on the topic, and present a thesis statement. Introductions can often be written in clever and creative ways. Bring in examples of interesting and unusual introductions you find in various pieces of writing, and have students discuss their effectiveness. In some introductions, writers start with an idea that is the opposite of the one they are actually going to develop and then transition into their actual thesis statement. They may explain why the topic is important, recount a brief story or incident, ask a provocative question, or use a quotation. Show students examples of these types of introductions. After they have completed a first draft, ask students to go back and write a completely new introduction for the paper, perhaps using a different technique. Then have them compare the two introductions and decide which one they think is stronger.

Have students use two different-colored highlighters or colored pencils. Ask them to use one color to highlight sections of their paper they feel are strong or well written. Use the other color to highlight areas that are weak and need improvement. This will help them to identify spots they need to revise.

This activity can help students improve the fluency of their papers: Have students read through one paragraph of their drafts and count the number of words in each sentence, writing down the number at the end of each. Then have them compare the numbers. Point out that most sentences are somewhere between fifteen and twenty-five words. Ideally, they want to have a few shorter sentences and some much longer sentences. This will help students identify if their sentences are short and choppy or too long and convoluted. If you and your students find this strategy helpful, then have them do it for all paragraphs throughout their papers.

Ask students to read their papers backward, beginning with the last sentence, then the next-to-last, and so forth. This practice forces the writer to look at each sentence in isolation and, rather than focusing on the content of the paper, instead focus on sentence structures. Writers are more likely to notice awkward and confusing sentences, run-ons, and incomplete sentences and fragments.

Have students study a particular paragraph in their essays and underline all of the verbs in the paragraph. Ask them to choose three verbs and replace them with stronger, more effective, or more vivid verbs (this might be a good time to study the vivid verbs activity in chapter 5). They should especially try to replace such weak verbs as *be* verbs, *put, take, make, do,* and *come* with stronger ones.

Have students read through their papers and focus on replacing vague and general nouns with more concrete ones, adding colorful adjectives and adverbs and sensory details, those that appeal to readers' sight, smell, taste, touch, or sound. Ask them to make sure they have details that appeal to at least three different senses.

Have students reread their drafts and identify three places where they can combine two or more sentences together into longer, more effective sentences. Sentence combining helps students eliminate chop-piness and build fluency and coherence in their writing.

Have students reread their papers and find three places where they can add an additional detail or example. Then have them make the necessary additions. This helps students build more effective and de-tailed support in their writing.

As busy teachers, we don't always have time to read and respond to students' rough drafts or conference with them individually about their drafts, but both of these strategies are highly effective. One technique you can use is reading quickly through students' drafts and making checkmarks in the margin whenever you find an error, problem, or poorly written part of the paper. Students should then go back and reassess that line or section to try to identify what the problem or error is. Individual conferencing with students is effective for both the revi-sion stage (evaluating content and style) as well as the editing stage (editing for sentence structure, punctuation, mechanics, and other con-ventions).

Having students focus on what they are doing well is important. Ask them to place a star in the margin next to what they think is the strong-est part of their paper. Have them use a highlighter to highlight the "golden words and phrases" in their papers.

Have students use a simple list of questions, such as the following, for revising their own and others' expository or explanatory writing:

- Identify the thesis statement of the essay. Is it clearly stated? If it is not stated, should it be?
- Does each paragraph have adequate and specific supporting de-tails and examples? Identify places where additional support could be added.
- Are there a number of transitional words and phrases to connect ideas?
- Does the essay have an interesting introduction? How could the introduction be rewritten to be more interesting?
- Does the writer use strong, active, and dynamic verbs?
- Who is the audience for the essay?
- Is the purpose of the essay clear, and does the format and style match the purpose? Is the purpose to define, describe, present a

process, analyze causes and effects, or discuss comparisons and contrasts?

- Does the writer include an adequate number of examples in the paper? Are they sufficient, relevant examples? Do they include facts, statistics, personal experiences, or other examples?
- Is the paper clearly and coherently organized? How could the organizational structure be improved?
- Are all the sentences complete and correct?
- Which errors in spelling, capitalization, grammar, usage, and punctuation can you identify?

The following is intended for more-advanced writers but might be adapted for other students, as well:

### Peer-Review Response Form for Essays

Writer of the paper:
Peer Reviewer:
Carefully read the student paper and answer the following questions in a thorough, detailed way:

1. What is your immediate response to the paper? What things did you like about the paper? What has the writer done well?
2. Does the paper have a clear thesis statement? What is it? Where is it located?
3. Is the paper well organized? What organizational method has the writer used? Is it effective?
4. Are there transitions in the paper? Do transitional words and phrases need to be added between sentences or paragraphs?
5. Is the paper sufficiently detailed? Point out parts where more details or examples could be included.
6. Has the writer used a rich, broad range of words? Is the vocabulary basic, good, or exceptional? What can the writer do to improve the word choice of the paper? Give examples.
7. Is there a variety of sentence structures and styles used in the paper? Is the paper smooth and easy to read? Point out any sentence fragments, run-on sentences, or places where the fluen-

cy of the paper is broken or the sentences could have more variety.

8. If the paper is making an argument, is the support for the argument clear and sufficient? Which additional evidence could be used?

9. Does the paper include cited material from sources? Is it cited correctly using MLA format? What corrections need to be made?

10. Consider the writer's use of conventions (punctuation, spelling, capitalization, or grammar). Which errors does the writer need to correct?

11. Does the paper demonstrate the writer's passion and commitment to the topic?

12. Reread both the introduction and conclusion. Are they strong and effective for the essay? How would you suggest they might be changed?

13. If this were your own paper and you were revising it, what would you change, add, or do differently?

—————

## KEY IDEAS IN THIS CHAPTER

- Common Core writing standard 2 addresses expository or informative/explanatory writing.
- Expository writing informs, explains, provides information, or describes, and it includes several different forms and patterns.
- Some expository writing requires research and note taking and may incorporate visual materials.
- Several strategies can be used to help students revise their writing for unity, coherence, and other elements.
- Peer-response strategies and forms can be used to help students assess their own and other students' writing.

# 5

# NARRATIVE WRITING

In general, narrative writing is writing that tells a story. It is one of the most common types of written communication, dating back to the earliest times when ancient peoples passed down stories and legends orally. Narratives appeal to us because people love hearing stories. People read novels and watch movies because they may want an escape from the reality of their own lives but also to gain insight into the human condition and vicariously experience the things that happen to others.

Fredricksen, Wilhelm, and Smith (2012) point out that "narratives help us understand and share where we come from" and are "especially important in helping us explore what is expected of us and how we might want to resist expectation" (p. 17). The narrative essay, in an academic context, is sometimes called a personal narrative, a story written about one's own personal experience or experiences.

Students with good imaginations may love to make up fictional stories, which is one type of narrative, but they may struggle more with developing an effective personal narrative. It is also important to note that narrative is often combined with other patterns of development. A student may be writing a comparison-contrast essay or a persuasive essay but may also find it useful to incorporate narrative elements. The following paragraphs present several important points about writing the personal narrative to keep in mind as we help students develop this genre.

First, the story presented in the narrative must have a purpose or theme. We generally don't just tell a story for the sake of telling a story;

rather, we tell it because we have an insight or a theme that we want to share. This central idea is often called the narrative point. We are sharing our own personal experiences in order to teach a lesson or a moral or share an insight or a lesson we have learned. As students begin planning for their narrative essays, ask them to clearly identify and even write down the narrative points they want to share.

It is also important to think about sequence when narrating a personal experience or event. Common Core writing standard 3c for grades 9 and 10 states that students must "[u]se a variety of techniques to sequence events so that they build on one another to create a coherent whole" (Council of Chief State School Officers and National Governors Association, 2010). Generally, stories are presented in chronological sequence, or in time order; however, encourage students to think about alternate methods of sequencing the story, such as flashback or flashforward. Would it make a more effective essay or help build suspense to start the story in the middle or even at the end and then flashback to the beginning? Also, as students are writing, have them refer to a list of transition words that show time order or sequence, such as *first, second, third, next, finally, previously, afterward,* and *as a result*.

Stories depend on conflict. If there is no conflict, then there is no plot. The conflict helps create the narrative tension that will keep the reader wanting to read until the end. In personal narratives, the conflict is often internal. For example, perhaps a student is writing a personal narrative about a time when she had to make a difficult decision. In this case, the conflict is going to come from the inner struggle she faces in trying to decide the best course of action to take. Have students clearly identify the conflicts in their narratives early in the writing process.

Common Core writing standard 3b for grades 9 and 10 states that students must "[u]se narrative techniques such as dialogue, pacing, description, reflection, and multiple plot lines, to develop experiences, events, and/or characters" (Council of Chief State School Officers and National Governors Association, 2010). Minilessons to teach each of these elements of plot development are helpful for students when they are working on narratives, as is having students read exemplar texts and models of narratives that use these elements.

One very important element that is difficult for students is using details selectively. Including irrelevant details that don't advance the story or the narrative point becomes tedious and boring for the reader. It is easy for young writers to get sidetracked and include too much detail that is irrelevant to the narrative (in some cases, to try to fill out the story to make it long enough to satisfy the requirements of the assignment). During the revision process, have students think about both aspects of the use of detail: Are there places where more specific detail needs to be included, and are there irrelevant details that don't advance the narrative and should be taken out?

Keeping the audience in mind during this process is important, as writers should be thinking about what the audience needs to know to understand the story. Students often ask whether *everything* in their narrative needs to be true. They also often ask what to do if they can't remember all the specific details, perhaps because the event they are recounting occurred a long time ago. Point out that, whenever people tell a story, orally or in writing, they often add details or supplement the plot with elements that may not have actually happened but that serve to make a better story.

Also point out to students that the readers will not know whether they have made up some of the details in the narrative. Writers often take dramatic license with their material and re-create events based on their memories of something that happened in the past. They select and reshape the events in order to build a good narrative.

One thing that you will need to spend some time teaching students while they are working on narrative papers is point of view and verb tense. Personal narratives are generally written in the first-person point of view, so, of course, students will need to use the personal *I* voice. When explaining how someone else may have viewed a particular event, the point of view may switch briefly to third person: "Suddenly, he saw the car careening around the corner."

Occasional use of the third person helps the writer to give some insight into how other people have seen and participated in the events. However, it is very important for writers to maintain a consistent verb tense. Inexperienced writers often begin their narratives in past tense and then switch to present tense for no reason, sometimes switching back and forth several times during their narratives. Tell students that, generally, we tell stories using past tense and that their verb tense throughout needs to be consistent. Provide students with a few examples of inconsistent verb tense, such as the following, and ask them to make necessary corrections:

> On Sunday, my friends and I went hiking. We walked all the way to the top of a big hill. I carried my backpack with all our supplies. When we got to the top, we find a big rock platform. It is right above a large pool of water where the river is wide. We decide to change our clothes and jump off the rock. My friend Pablo jumps in first and then I follow him. He jumps headfirst, but I am afraid the water is not deep enough. We had so much fun climbing onto the rocks and cooling off in the refreshing water.

In this passage, the writer appropriately begins telling the story in past tense, with such verbs as *went*, *walked*, and *carried*. Then the verb tense abruptly changes with the present-tense verbs *find*, *is*, and *decide*. At the end of the passage, the verb tense switches back to past tense. Present examples like this one or excerpts from students' papers, and ask students to identify the problems with verb tense.

Another important point is that students often have a hard time choosing a topic for a narrative and may feel that they don't really have any significant experiences to share that would be interesting to readers. Remind them that good narratives can be written about almost anything; their stories do not have to feature some exotic locale or recount earth-shattering events.

The effectiveness of the narrative lies in the writer's desire to share an experience with the reader and the use of details to develop the narrative. Fredricksen, Wilhelm, and Smith (2012) present an activity (paraphrased here) designed to help students reflect on their own lives and on the events that shaped them:

- Students free-write for five to fifteen minutes about their life stories, beginning with birth and ending with present day. They write "I was born" on the top of the page and "I sit in class writing my life story" on the bottom of the page. This step gives students a chance to reflect and learn more about themselves in order to help identify a moment they want to focus more closely on.
- After their free-writing, students read what they wrote and circle or highlight one incident they want to explore more.

- Next, students write more (another ten minutes or so) about their memory of that moment, including such details as who was there; what they were doing; what happened; where it took place; what they remember seeing, smelling, hearing, and feeling; and what they wanted in that moment.

Another crucial aspect of good narrative writing is use of descriptive detail. Common Core writing standard 3d for grades 9 and 10 states that students should "[u]se precise words and phrases, telling details, and sensory language to convey a vivid picture of the experiences, events, setting, and/or characters" (Council of Chief State School Officers and National Governors Association, 2010).

Effectively using specific detail in narrative writing is challenging for most students. Discuss with students the difference between telling and showing. Writers depend on both telling and showing the reader what happened, but students frequently rely mostly on details that tell the reader what happened. Details that show are those that create immediacy, create a picture in the reader's head, and appeal to the reader's senses.

Choose some examples of writing from essays and literary fiction or nonfiction that illustrate details that show. Have students identify and discuss the specific details the writers use in the passages. Another strategy is to give students some examples of telling sentences (for example, "The boy walked down the hallway.") and ask them to practice rewriting them with details that show: "The tall, lanky young man with dirty-blond hair, worn jeans, and an oversize sweatshirt dragged himself slowly down the dark hallway, shuffling his feet, his eyes downcast, looking aimless and sad."

This type of rich, descriptive detail is what brings writing to life and will add immensely to students' narrative papers once they have learned to use it in their own writing. The next step, of course, is to ask students to identify sentences in their rough drafts that are telling sentences and try rewriting them with details that show.

In her book *Blowing away the State Writing Assessment Test*, Jane Bell Kiester (2006) presents several excellent strategies for teaching students to write "vivid-verb paragraphs," where the first sentence is a telling sentence, the middle sentences use only strong verbs, and the last sentence provides a conclusion. She first teaches students to avoid "dead" and "dying" verbs and presents a list of common dead verbs, such as forms of the *be* verb; verbs ending in *-ing*; and such sense verbs as *looks, feels, smells,* and *sounds.* Her technique then requires students to practice rewriting several sentences, replacing the dead verbs with strong verbs. Based on Kiester's (2006) strategy, the following assignment sheet gives students direction in writing vivid-verb paragraphs.

———✦✦✦———

### Vivid-Verb Paragraphs

What is a "vivid-verb paragraph"? It is a paragraph composed of five to seven sentences that use strong verbs. It should adhere to the following format:

**Sentence 1:** A "telling" sentence. This sentence is the paragraph's topic sentence and states the main point of the paragraph. Example: "The movie *Dark Night Rises* is a really good movie."

**Sentences 2 through 6 (or 8):** All of these sentences in the middle of the paragraph use only strong, vivid verbs with no verbs used more than once. None of the verbs may be "dead or dying" verbs, such as forms of the *be* verb—no *is, was,* or *were.* Underline the verbs in each sentence to make sure they are vivid verbs. Use transition words between sentences.

**Last sentence:** A conclusion sentence that does not repeat the first sentence but can be similar to it. It may also use a "telling" verb.

On a piece of paper, write the topic of your paragraph at the top of the page. In the middle of the page, draw a circle. Write your topic sentence inside the circle. Draw four to six cluster sentences around the outside of the topic sentence. Draw a line from each one to the topic sentence circle. Number each one in the order you will include it in the paragraph. At the bottom of the page, write your concluding sentence.

Next, write out your full vivid-verb paragraph on a new sheet of paper in ink. Underline the verb in each sentence, and make sure the middle sentences all have vivid verbs.

Here is an example of a vivid-verb paragraph. Notice the strong verbs in bold:

> The dog at the shelter was very funny. It **leaped** around, **chasing** its tail, but of course, it never **caught** it. The dog **whined** and **howled**, **dashing** around after the ball. It **stopped**, **stared** intently, and

**barked** loudly. Its tail **wagged** and **flipped** like a flag in the wind. A funny expression **flashed** across its furry face. The dog was so hysterical, I **decided** to adopt it and take it home.

—◦◦◦◦—

Also, provide students with several other examples of vivid-verb paragraphs. This process requires lots of practice for students to master, but eventually, the quality of the verbs they use in their writing improves.

One way to help students improve their use of good descriptive detail and help them to create writing that "shows" rather than tells is to teach them to write details that appeal to the different senses. Use the five-senses chart in Figure 5.1 or have students draw the chart on a piece of paper.

Illustrate this process by having the entire class complete the five-senses chart for a particular location, perhaps one that your particular students would have some experience with. In the Pacific Northwest, as well as in other parts of the country, for example, most students have visited the beach. However, the five-senses chart can be used for any descriptive topic.

Have the class brainstorm as many details as possible to fill in each column of the chart: sight, sound, touch, taste, and smell. For example, using the topic of the beach, in the sound column, students might come up with the following details:

- The cry of seagulls
- The waves crashing against the beach
- The laughter and screams of children playing
- The visitors splashing in the water
- The dogs barking
- The sand crunching under your feet

For the sense of touch, they might come up with the following:

- The gritty sand
- The biting sting of the cold wind and rain hitting your face
- The cold water splashing around your ankles
- The moist sand squeezing between your toes

Location/Setting:_____

| Sight | Sound | Touch | Taste | Smell |
|-------|-------|-------|-------|-------|
|       |       |       |       |       |
|       |       |       |       |       |
|       |       |       |       |       |
|       |       |       |       |       |

Figure 5.1.  Five-senses chart

- The hard, cold, smooth beach rocks

For the sense of smell, students might come up with the salty, briny air; the fishy odor; the smell of wood smoke; the delicious smells of nearby food carts; and for taste they might list the salty taste of seawater splashing and the gritty taste of sand blowing into your mouth. Because we depend on the sense of sight most, students can probably generate a long list of details about what we might see at the beach.

After modeling use of the five-senses chart with the whole class, have students complete a five-senses chart for the settings of their own narratives. Have them refer to their chart as they are writing their papers in order to try to work in all the details.

The following is a similar activity to help students learn and practice writing good descriptive detail. It includes example sentences from *The Longman Reader* (Nadell, Langan, & Comodromos, 2009).

—⟨⟨⟩⟩—

## Descriptive Detail

Note: Example sentences from Judith Nadell, John Langan, and Eliza A. Comodromos's *The Longman Reader*, 9th ed. Reprinted by permission of Pearson Education, Inc., New York.

What you must learn: Good writing shows rather than tells. Good writers use a lot of descriptive detail and sensory impressions. Add specific detail to your writing and appeal to the readers' senses:

- Sight
- Smell
- Sound
- Taste
- Touch

Your details should create a picture in the readers' minds, the same one you have in your head as you are writing. Here are some examples:

> **Vague:** The food was disgusting. The car moved slowly down the road.
>
> **Specific:** The greasy bowl of stew, filled with rancid meat and lumps of mushy vegetables, congealed into an oval pool of milky-brown fat. Burdened with its load of clamoring children and well-worn suitcases, the Chevrolet Malibu labored down the highway on bald tires and worn shocks, emitting puffs of blue exhaust and an occasional backfire.

Using concrete, sensory-filled sentences creates vivid word pictures that are engaging. It makes writing interesting! Figures of speech, such as metaphors and similes, also add to descriptive detail, as do strong verbs. Notice the verbs in the following examples:

- Moving as jerkily as a marionette on strings, the old man *picked* himself up off the sidewalk and *staggered* down the street.
- *Stalking* their prey, the hall monitors *remained* hidden in the corridors, motionless and ready to *spring* on any unsuspecting student sneaking into class late.
- The scoop of vanilla ice cream, plain and unadorned, *cried out* for hot-fudge sauce and a sprinkling of sliced pecans.

Exercise: Take two of the following "telling" sentences and rewrite them with one or more sentences using lots of descriptive detail. Use a simile or metaphor in one of your revised versions:

- The beach was nice.
- The party was fun.
- The football game was great.
- The garden was relaxing.

—————

Another important element that adds to the effectiveness of students' narrative writing is the use of dialogue. Students can often make their papers much more interesting and realistic by re-creating some dialogue in the story. When teaching narrative writing, always include a review of the punctuation rules of using dialogue:

- Start a new paragraph every time the speaker changes.
- Dialogue tags, such as "he said" or "she stated," can be used; however, if you are writing a long conversation between two people, the dialogue tags can be left out.
- For indirect quotes, don't use quotation marks, as in "He told me he would be coming by later."
- If the person's words include a question, statement, or command, then place the correct punctuation mark inside the final quotation mark: He asked, "Why are these assignments always so hard?"

- When the sentence is interrupted by a dialogue tag, use a comma before and after the tag: "Tell me," she demanded, "how you expect to go to school wearing those clothes."
- If the entire sentence asks a question, but the quote itself does not, the question mark should be placed outside the quote marks: Didn't I just hear the teacher say, "The test will be tomorrow"?
- If one person is quoted for more than two paragraphs, use a quote mark at the beginning of each paragraph and at the end of the last paragraph.

It's also a good idea with dialogue to teach students to use a variety of dialogue tags so that they don't just use "he said" and "she said" repeatedly. Provide students with a list of other possible dialogue tags: *insisted, proclaimed, announced, stated, whispered, exclaimed, ordered, demanded, agreed, commented, denied, mentioned, repeated, snapped, chortled, sputtered,* and *muttered.* As a useful classroom exercise, take a passage of dialogue from a novel, and remove all the dialogue tags. Then ask students to identify various tags that could be used in the dialogue.

Another useful activity is to hand each student a copy of a novel. Ask them to find passages in the novel that use dialogue and then generate a list of all the verbs that writers use in writing dialogue. Another good practice activity for dialogue is to present students with two characters and ask them to write a conversation between them in the form of an extended dialogue. For example: a conversation between a ninth-grade student who has cheated on a test and his teacher or a young girl and her mother on their way to Disneyland.

Fredricksen, Wilhelm, and Smith (2012, p. 50) also present a useful strategy for descriptive detail, dialogue, and characterization in narrative writing, which is adapted here:

1. Have students create a group of characters, five or more, or you can supply a list of characters for students.
2. Students choose one of the characters and place the character in a confined physical space, such as in an automobile or on an elevator, or an emotional space, such as a feeling of longing, restlessness, or loneliness.

3. Students introduce a second character, someone in a position of power over the main character—a coach, an elder, a relative—or someone who has an annoying habit whom the main character will interact with.
4. Have students write for ten minutes, reporting what happens in the exchange between the two characters.
5. Students share what they have written with a partner.
6. Students then write for ten more minutes only using dialogue between the two characters.
7. Students share with a partner.
8. Students then write for fifteen minutes, combining action and dialogue.
9. Students share with a partner again.
10. Students then find two places to add what the character is thinking and add details that describe the story world or setting without naming the place itself.

This type of activity provides good practice for students to develop narrative techniques they can apply to their own writing.

Brooks (2007) uses short pieces of text with descriptive detail and shares them with students as examples. Then, students are asked to write a "detailed description of two people eating together. From the description, the readers should get a sense of who the people are, their relationship to each other, circumstances under which they are eating." In this exercise, students are asked to use as many details as possible, describing clothing, smells, mannerisms of the characters, and hairstyles. The people described might be grandparents, homeless people, two friends, and so forth (p. 11).

Students' success in writing good narrative papers often lies in the teacher providing good prompts and allowing students to choose from a number of different prompts. Here is a list of possible general topics for narrative essays that you may find useful:

• Write a narrative about a day that was special to you for some reason.
• Write about a time in your life that involved one of the following: surprise, discovery, sadness, or survival. Tell the story of what happened.

- Think about a time when you faced a challenge. Write a personal narrative about the time that explains what happened, how you dealt with the challenge, and the outcome.
- Write a story about a time when you taught something to someone else. Tell the story using a clear sequence of events to show what happened.
- Think about a time in your life when you learned an important lesson. Write a narrative about what happened and what lesson you learned.
- Write a narrative about your best holiday celebration ever.
- Write about a time in your life when you were affected by some kind of weather event. Use narrative structure that builds suspense, and include lots of details about what happened.
- Write about a time when you did something that made you feel good. Perhaps when you helped the team win, did something nice for someone else, or participated in a group effort. It could be something you had never done before. Be sure to explain what happened and why you felt good about it afterward.
- Write about a vivid memory from your childhood. Explain all the events that you can remember in a sequence that will help readers understand the event.
- Write about a time when you achieved a personal goal, and tell the story of finally meeting that goal.
- Write a personal narrative about one of the following events: a memorable wedding, a funeral, a football game, your first day at a new school, your first day on a new job, an embarrassing experience, a journey, a memorable experience, a breakup, a vacation, a dangerous experience, an act of heroism, a vacation, an accident, or an unexpected encounter.

Have students use the following checklist to respond to their own and other students' drafts:

- Is there a clear narrative point in the introduction? Does the writer provide a reason he or she is telling the story?
- Does each paragraph have adequate supporting details?
- Is there adequate descriptive detail? Where in the paper could the writer include more narrative detail?

- Does the writing show rather than just tell the story?
- Does the paper use good, strong, active, vivid verbs?
- Does the story take place within a sufficiently limited time frame?
- Does the writer maintain a consistent point of view, either in past or present tense?
- Does the writer use dialogue to develop the story? Locate some places where the writer might include some dialogue.
- Are there transitional words and phrases used that show the passage of time?
- Does the paper have an interesting introduction that draws the reader into the story?
- Does the paper have a conclusion? How could the conclusion be improved so that it draws the narrative to an effective close?
- Are all the sentences complete and correct? If the writer uses fragments, are they effectively used for stylistic purposes?
- Can you identify any errors in spelling, punctuation, capitalization, grammar, or usage that the writer needs to correct?

## KEY IDEAS IN THIS CHAPTER

- Narrative writing in academic contexts is usually called personal narrative, a story about one's own experiences.
- Narratives must have a purpose or theme, a sequence, a conflict, and selectively used details.
- Narratives should maintain a consistent point of view and verb tense.
- Narratives depend on specific descriptive detail, and many strategies can be used to teach students to use good details, including vivid-verb paragraphs and the five-senses chart.
- Narratives may also incorporate passages of dialogue to add to the realism and effectiveness of the writing.

# 6

# ARGUMENT WRITING

**A**rgument writing, or argumentation, is used in many different contexts and for a variety of purposes, both in academic disciplines and in real-world contexts. There is a wealth of material we can teach our students to help them learn the principles of effective argumentation.

We need to begin by teaching them that the word *argument*, in academic contexts, does not refer to a fight or disagreement. It is not a battle or a confrontation but rather a piece of writing or some other form of communication that tries to convince readers to accept a particular position or opinion, often about a controversial issue. In some cases, we may also want to make a proposal and encourage readers to take some form of action. In academic writing, argumentation is the centerpiece of intellectual debate and discussion. Andrews (2009) notes that argument "refers to the most highly prized type of academic discourse: something that is deemed essential to a thesis, to an article in a research journal, to a dissertation, essay, and to many other kinds of writing within schools and the academy" (p. 1).

Adolescent writers need direct instruction in the cognitive strategies and rhetorical techniques that will help them learn to craft effective written arguments on a variety of academic topics. Most scholars view argumentation, which relies primarily on logical support to make its case, as being fundamentally different from persuasion, which depends more on emotional appeals and appealing to readers' values and ideals. However, the distinction between argument and persuasion is not particularly useful, especially for middle or high school writers in basic-level writing courses. The reality is that writers typically rely on both argumentation and persuasion strategies in developing their pieces. People respond to arguments using logic as well as emotion, so the thoughtful writer is naturally going to appeal to both. Emotional appeals should complement the logic of the argument but not replace it, of course.

The Greek philosopher Aristotle originally identified three central rhetorical elements of arguments, whether spoken or written: logos, pathos, and ethos. Logos refers to the logic and sound reasoning of your position, which depends on your use of good evidence and support. Pathos refers to the emotional appeal to the readers' needs, values, and ideals. Writers use language effectively to appeal to the readers' emotions. Ethos refers to the writer's credibility and integrity. It involves convincing readers that you are knowledgeable about your topic, that you have good intentions, and that you are not making the argument only for selfish reasons but are concerned about the greater good. Inflammatory language and overemotionalism will undercut the writer's credibility.

One important element of argument writing is that it typically addresses a topic that is controversial in some way. An effective argument also anticipates the opposing viewpoints and counterclaims and addresses or refutes those effectively. If you are writing an argument in favor of school uniforms, then you need to consider the reasons some people object to school systems requiring students to wear school uniforms. Perhaps some readers believe strongly that one's individual style of dress is an important aspect of self-expression and that being required to wear a uniform is a violation of their free speech and freedom to express themselves. You need to not only acknowledge these objections in your essay but also address them, explaining why self-expression and free speech often must be limited or curtailed in public or private school settings in order to maintain order, promote equality, and keep the focus on learning.

The Common Core State Standards (CCSS), as well as most other state language arts standards, address argument writing. In the CCSS anchor standards for writing, argumentation is addressed in the very first standard: "Write arguments to support claims in an analysis of substantive topics or texts, using valid reasoning and relevant and sufficient evidence" (Council of Chief State School Officers and National

Governors Association, 2010). Let's examine the specific subpoints of the argument writing standard for grades 9 and 10:

1. Introduce precise claim(s), distinguish the claim(s) from alternate or opposing claims, and create an organization that establishes clear relationships among claim(s), counterclaims, reasons, and evidence.
2. Develop claim(s) and counterclaims fairly, supplying evidence for each while pointing out the strengths and limitations of both in a manner that anticipates the audience's knowledge level and concerns.
3. Use words, phrases, and clauses to link the major sections of the text, create cohesion, and clarify the relationships between claim(s) and reasons, between reasons and evidence, and between claim(s) and counterclaims.
4. Establish and maintain a formal style and objective tone while attending to the norms and conventions of the discipline in which they are writing.
5. Provide a concluding statement or section that follows from and supports the argument presented.

Teachers might consider developing miniunits for each of these particular subpoints. You will need to teach students about claims and how to write and develop good claims for argument pieces, as well as how to address counterclaims. Subpoint 2 addresses the use of evidence, and students may need some help in learning about different types of evidence and how to identify the strengths and limitations of evidence in order to identify the best evidence for their arguments. Subpoint 3 addresses transitional words and phrases and how to organize the text in a way that creates cohesion and clarifies relationships. Subpoint 4 addresses style and tone. Students may need some lessons to help them learn to use academic language and an appropriate tone. And finally, subpoint 5 addresses conclusions. For many writers, the conclusion is the most difficult part of an essay to write. You may want to help students generate a list of effective concluding techniques for essays and discuss which ones may be most effective for argument essays. Use sample argument essays, and have students analyze and compare the various ways that writers conclude their arguments.

Argument essays often require students to do more prewriting and planning for their essays. Consider requiring students to complete outlines that you can check prior to beginning the rough drafts of their papers. Figure 6.1 presents the planning sheet for argument essays. Have students complete this format in the beginning stages of the writing process and while they are doing some preliminary research and gathering ideas for their essays.

You might want to spend some time discussing outlining with students because number 9 asks them to create an outline. It's particularly important to teach outlining in the context of argument writing because it is a genre that requires careful organization and preplanning in order to write an effective essay. The most common type of outline is called the alphanumeric outline, one that uses a combination of letters and numbers that are arranged in the following heading levels: Roman numerals for major headings, capital letters for subheadings, and then Arabic numerals and lowercase letters for the remaining levels.

Outlines can also be very simple topic outlines or more detailed sentence outlines. For topic outlines, each major heading and subheading is just topics, short phrases, or labels; in sentence outlines, each major heading and subheading is a complete sentence.

Some teachers require that the thesis statement be placed at the top of the outline. Also, outlines must not contain single division; in other words, if there is an A, then there must also be a B. There cannot be only a 1 without a 2 or 3, either. All common heading levels should be carefully lined up underneath one another. Use Figure 6.2 to teach students correct alphanumeric outline format, and consider asking them to prepare an outline when planning for an argument essay.

## STRATEGIES FOR TEACHING ARGUMENT

This section presents several suggestions and strategies for teaching the principles of argument writing.

### Understanding Different Types of Audiences

It is important for students to recognize that, anytime they face a situation where they need to make an argument, the success of their argu-

1. General topic of the essay: _____

2. Narrowed topic of the essay: _____

3. In the space below, write your thesis statement for the essay. Remember, a thesis statement must be a *statement*, not a question, not a summary, not a topic, and not an announcement:

4. Below, list several pieces of evidence you will include to support your claim:

5. Write a preliminary idea for a title, keeping in mind that you can always change it later:

6. Write down a couple counterarguments that you may need to address or refute in your essay:

7. Describe how you will introduce the topic in an interesting way that draws the reader into the paper. What effective hook or grabber will you use in your introduction (a quotation, anecdote, startling fact, etc.)?

8. Does the paper describe a problem, and if so, what possible solution to the problem will you present?

9. On another piece of paper, carefully outline your essay before you begin writing a rough draft.

**Figure 6.1. Planning sheet for argument essays**

I. Introduction
   A. Background information
   B. Thesis
II. Main idea 1
   A. Supporting idea 1
      1. Subtopic
      2. Subtopic
      3. Subtopic
   B. Supporting idea 2
      1. Subtopic
      2. Subtopic
   C. Supporting idea 3
      1. Subtopic
         a. Example or detail
         b. Example or detail
         c. Example or detail
      2. Subtopic
         a. Example or detail
         b. Example or detail
      3. Subtopic
III. Main idea 2
   A. Supporting idea 1
      1. Subtopic
      2. Subtopic
   B. Supporting idea 2
      1. Subtopic
      2. Subtopic
IV. Main idea 3
V. Conclusion

**Figure 6.2.   Alphanumeric outline format**

ment may depend on the type of audience they will have. If you are asking students to write authentically and for a real-world audience or purpose, then they will need to try to analyze their readers and perhaps alter their approaches to their topics and support based on the type of audiences they face. Ask them to consider how much their audiences may already know about their topics, how they will feel about their arguments, and what their needs and values may be.

Audiences may be supportive, indifferent, or hostile to an argument. If the audience is supportive, then the writer might need to focus less on use of detailed evidence and instead use stronger emotional appeals to capitalize on the readers' commitment to the topic and perhaps convince them to take action. An indifferent or undecided audience may already be somewhat informed about the topic or issue but will need lots of evidence, facts, and supporting reasons to persuade them.

The writer will also have to carefully establish her credibility (ethos) on the topic. A hostile or skeptical audience will obviously be the most difficult to persuade. This type of audience will require lots of logical support and evidence in support of the argument, and they are not likely to respond well to emotional appeals. The best you can do with a hostile audience may be to simply get them to think about the issue or perhaps be more willing to compromise or find a middle-ground position in the argument.

## Writing an Effective Claim

A thesis statement expresses the controlling idea of an essay, the central point or idea the author wants to make. When the paper is an argument essay, the thesis statement is generally called a claim, the position that you have formulated on a controversial topic and that you hope to defend in your essay. The claim is usually expressed in one and sometimes two sentences that describe the main idea of the paper and the argument you are making. In some cases, it may offer a preview of your subpoints, but it is important that it focuses the paper on a specific and debatable point.

Teach students to think of the claim as the following three-part formula: claim + reason = thesis or controlling idea. The claim is the assertion you are making, but a good claim statement also offers some main reason or support for the claim. For example, your thesis is

"Biased content in high school history textbooks is harmful." This thesis states the argument, but to make a stronger thesis, it needs to identify a central reason: "because it advances certain political agendas, promotes negative stereotypes, and limits the contributions of many groups."

Here is another example: "Many women suffer from eating disorders" is a factual statement rather than an argument. The statement is true, but it is not an arguable assertion. Here's a better claim statement: "Advertising and media influence how women view themselves and how they behave, and media can lead to harmful behaviors, such as eating disorders."

Sometimes a claim statement also includes a call to action. Here is an example: "The federal government should support early childhood education by providing the resources for local communities to open more day care centers." This type of claim is often called a claim of policy because the writer is recommending specific policy changes that should be made.

Sometimes, students will try to write a question, a fact, or an announcement rather than a claim or thesis. Teach your students that a claim must be a one- or two-sentence statement, not a question. A good thesis is also *not* a statement that merely presents factual information, such as the earlier example, because if it is a fact, then there is no argument to make. Writers must also avoid making an announcement, such as, "This paper will discuss the death penalty" or "I am going to write about why recycling should be mandatory."

One way to have students practice using claims is with print or online advertisements. Advertisements are an abbreviated form of an argument, as are numerous other types of multimodal communication. Have students practice identifying claim and support by analyzing a printed advertisement. You can make this project a written or oral assignment.

Have students work with a partner to examine a few magazines for an advertisement to use for the assignment. Ask them to analyze the ad and its various components and then identify the claim and the support made. If you have also taught students how to identify the warrant of an argument, then you can ask them to try to identify the warrant (an assumption underlying the argument and providing a bridge between claim and support). Then, have them present the ad to the class, explaining claim, support, and warrant.

## Planning

The first step in writing a good argument essay is choosing an appropriate topic, of course. In some cases, you might assign students a particular general topic or ask them to choose from a list of topics. If they are allowed to have free choice, then they might begin by skimming through newspapers and online articles or editorials and jotting down a list of topics they find interesting. Help students to identify topics that they care about because if they are passionate about certain topics or issues, then they will be more likely to write compelling and effective arguments.

Students can also generate some topic ideas by brainstorming with a partner or small group. After choosing a topic and doing some preliminary reading or research, they will need to decide which aspects or issues related to their topics they want to address in order to identify their claims. Have students actually write out their claim statements and spend some time working with them to make sure all students have a solid claim they can defend, one that is neither too narrow nor too broad.

## Gathering Evidence

Next, ask students to think through the rhetorical situation: task, audience, and purpose. The next step in the planning process is to have students consider different viewpoints of the issue and begin gathering evidence and examples from different sources. You might have them make a two-column list of evidence to support their claims and evidence to support counterclaims. Evidence can include facts, informed opinions, statistics, and reasons. Evidence is stronger if it comes from a reliable, unbiased source, and for some argument topics, if it is current and up to date.

The next step is to organize and structure the argument. Students should review all points of support they have collected, rank them in terms of their importance or effectiveness, and arrange them in an emphatic way (least important to most important). Have students create an outline or use some other type of graphic organizer to lay out the structure of their essays (see Figure 6.2). Students can also prepare an organizational chart that will help them plan each of the three parts of their essays:

1. **Introduction:** Grabs the reader's attention (a hook) and states claim
2. **Body:** Presents multiple paragraphs with several pieces of supporting evidence, refutes the opposing viewpoints, and uses lots of details and examples to develop each point
3. **Conclusion:** Follows from and supports the argument, restates the claim, and may make a recommendation or call to action

## Refuting the Opposition

Writers will need to consider their claims carefully and review the lists of counterclaims they made earlier. When students are writing about complex issues, they may need to spend some time refuting the counterclaims, or arguments on the opposite side of the issue. The refutation of counterclaims is sometimes called rebuttal. Have them practice this process by using sentence frames, such as the following: "While some readers might argue that [fill in the blank], I disagree with this approach because [fill in the blank]." Good rebuttals of counterclaims will make a stronger argument essay.

Suppose students are writing an argument that claims that parents should be able to choose which schools their children attend. Students might begin by noting that freedom of choice is a treasured value in our society and that, in an ideal world, it would be nice if everyone could choose which school they wanted to attend. Then, the writer would need to go on to show how logistically this freedom of choice would lead to an unmanageable situation for school districts.

Students could present statistics and discuss how students are assigned to particular schools based on school district boundaries and in a manner that fairly balances the student population of each school. The process students would follow for any argument should be a three-part process:

1. State the claim
2. Acknowledge counterclaims and opposing viewpoints
3. Refute the opposing viewpoints by presenting counterarguments

Figure 6.3 shows a graphic organizer and planning sheet you can use to help students to prepare their essays.

## Using Logic and Avoiding Fallacies

While an in-depth study of deductive and inductive reasoning and logical fallacies is best reserved for advanced groups of students and college writing courses, you may want to introduce some basic types of logical fallacies in the context of argument writing. Recognizing logical fallacies helps writers learn to avoid faulty logic in their own writing, as well as to expose them in counterclaims. Here are some common logical fallacies:

**Topic**: _____

**Claim**: _____

_____

| Supporting Evidence | Counterclaim | Refutation/Rebuttal |
|---|---|---|
| #1 | | |
| #2 | | |
| #3 | | |
| #4 | | |

**Figure 6.3. Argument evidence planning chart**

**Post-hoc fallacy** (from the Latin *post hoc ergo propter hoc,* or "After this, therefore because of this") is when one event occurs after another, leading one to believe that the first event caused the second. In reality, no cause–effect relationship may be present at all. This fallacy can lead to a chain of faulty thinking.

**Nonsequitur** ("It does not follow") is when one draws a conclusion that has little or no connection to the evidence cited. For example, "Lots of people own cars, so there is no need to provide funding for city buses." The faulty conclusion overlooks the many people who don't own cars or who cannot drive. It also ignores possible environmental concerns created by too many cars on the road.

**Begging the question** is when the writer fails to provide proof of an arguable point, expecting the readers to merely accept the argument as is. For example, "People who commit murder should receive the death penalty because they are killers who have taken someone else's life."

**False analogy** presents a comparison between two unlike things that may be similar in some ways; the fallacious analogy assumes that they are alike in every way, which is likely not true. While the digestive system and a car's engine may be similar in one or two aspects, they are completely different in many other ways.

**Ad hominem fallacy** is a personal attack on someone; that is, attacking the person based on their personal characteristics, history, and background rather than focusing on the issue or argument at hand. One can find many examples of this in politics.

**Red herring** is an intentional attempt to distract the reader's attention from the matter at hand by making a digression. For example, a young person asks her mother for a raise in her allowance, and her mother replies, "Well, you're lucky. When I was your age, I only got a dollar a week."

**Slippery slope** is the assumption that taking one step will lead to a more significant event, which in turn leads to another more significant event, and so on, until there is some ultimate negative effect. The implication that one action will inevitably lead to a series of others is fallacious, and each is increasingly improbable. For example, "If we allow people of the same sex to marry, then soon people will want to marry their siblings, their pets, or their cars."

There are many online resources for teaching fallacies and an abundance of examples of fallacies. You might present some examples to students and have them work in small groups to identify and explain the fallacious reasoning.

## Writing and Revising

Students will need some time to devote to writing the first drafts of their papers. Using their outlines, charts, or notes in the previous stages, they should begin by writing introductions that introduce the claims and not only clearly present their positions on their topics but also convince readers of the topics' importance.

You may want to conference with students about their introductions and give them suggestions for improving the opening paragraphs before having them move onto the body section. It is also a good idea to teach students some different strategies for writing good introductions. Most importantly, an introduction should draw the readers into the topic and should interest readers so that they will want to keep reading.

The following are all good ways to introduce an argument essay: start with a brief anecdote or story that relates to the argument, include a surprising or shocking statistic or fact, start with a quotation from an expert or source, tell a personal story or relate an experience that called the writer's attention to the topic, provide background information that provides a larger context for the topic, define key concepts and terms that readers will need to understand, appeal to the readers' interests and values, or start with a thought-provoking question. And, of course, the introduction must include the thesis and may also provide a preview of the writer's major pieces of supporting evidence.

Next, following their outlines, students will write the bodies of their papers, developing their supporting points with plenty of evidence, quotations, and examples. It is especially important to help students find and develop appropriate supporting evidence that is detailed and specific. Use the transitions lists and activities presented earlier to help students with organizing and transitioning between paragraphs.

Finally, have students write concluding paragraphs that follow logically from their body sections, and if appropriate, make a recommendation or ask the readers to take action. When students have a completed draft, it is important to provide them with some opportunities to get feedback on it from other readers. If possible, conference with students individually about their drafts. Also, have them exchange their drafts with another student and use the checklist provided in this section or some other tool to give each other suggestions and feedback.

Depending on your class, you may want to arrange students into peer-response groups and have them read their papers aloud to the group to get feedback and suggestions from their peers. Provide students with some sentence starters to help them offer appropriate responses to their fellow students. For example, "One thing you have done really well is [fill in the blank]"; "One place where you need more explanation is [fill in the blank]"; "One section where I was confused is [fill in the blank]"; "The things you need to do to improve the paper are [fill in the blank]."

The next stage of the writing process is revising and improving the paper, making sure it is clear, coherent, and interesting. During the revision process, use minilessons to help students practice sentence combining; using transitions; elaborating on evidence; and improving word choice, introductions, and conclusions.

Have students read their essays out loud to themselves during the revision process. This is one of the most valuable techniques that any writer can use to improve their writing. At the end of the writing process, students will need to spend some time revising and editing. This would be a good time to include minilessons on conventions to focus on correct sentence structures, spelling, capitalization, punctuation, and grammar.

## Appropriate Style and Tone

For many writers, especially younger ones, one of the hardest aspects of argument writing may be learning to use an appropriately formal style and tone. Students need to learn that we generally don't write with the same level of informality with which we speak; writing, especially argument writing, is much more formal. Whether the tone is more objective or more subjective, the writing style should still be formal. Use the strategies in chapter 2 to help students improve the word choice and language of their essays.

Also, teach students to use such transitional words and phrases such as *for this reason, therefore, on the other hand, consequently, on the contrary*, and *for example* to add formality to writing. Have students go through their drafts to identify such general words and terms as *lots*, *things*, *stuff*, and *everything*, as well as any slang or colloquial terms that are not appropriate in formal writing, and rewrite these informal sentences to make them more formal. Teach students to elevate their level of diction: Instead of "cool things," use "clever and cunning approaches." Instead of "The house was fancy," use "The country mansion was elaborately decorated and opulent."

Students should also work on combining sentences, as one aspect of a more formal writing style is longer and more sophisticated sentence structure. Help them practice combining short, disconnected sentences (as well as avoiding fragments and run-ons). For example, "The school is losing money. It is buying unnecessary supplies," can be revised as "The school is losing money because it is buying unnecessary supplies."

Here is another simple example: "Lots of schools have energy-conservation programs. Lincoln High School has a great energy-conservation program. The program is run by the Environmental Club." This can be revised as "Many schools, including Lincoln High School, have great energy-conservation programs, several of which are run by an environmental club or other student group."

## Using Models of Good Argument Essays

One of the most effective ways to teach writing is to use models. It is important to show students what a good essay looks like and to have them read and discuss a number of example pieces. This is true with argument writing, as well. Over time, you can collect examples from your students, but you can also find many great models online and in the real world. Keep a collection of good editorials and argument pieces from newspapers, magazine columns, and online sources on a variety of topics.

If your school is an AVID school, then you have access to *AVID Weekly* (www.avidweekly.org), which is a great source of informational and argumentative articles and editorials from a variety of sources. Check with an administrator or your school's AVID coordinator for a user name and password. A *New York Times* online subscription also gives you access to many examples of excellent writing and editorials, as does Newsela (https://newsela.com).

## Writing Arguments about Literary Text

This type of writing is often called literary analysis or critique. It is a formal response to a piece of literature—story, poem, play, or novel—in which the writer defends his or her interpretation of the literary work using logical reasoning and strong support. The basic elements of good argument writing apply to literary analysis, as well. In most cases you are probably going to ask students to write an analysis of a particular aspect or element of the work, such as author's style, theme, conflict, point of view, characters, or some other literary element.

For literary analysis, students will need to write a thesis statement or claim for this type of writing and include possible counterclaims to address opposing interpretations; textual evidence, including examples and quotes from the piece; good organization, style, and tone; and accuracy. If you are allowing students some choice in which aspect of the work they choose to analyze, help them begin by choosing an aspect to focus on.

Perhaps they want to prove that the text is the best piece by that particular author or in that particular genre or analyze the motivations of a particular character in the story. Perhaps their purpose is to analyze the sound effects used by the poet or the dramatic irony used by the playwright. Have students write out a statement of purpose: "In this essay, I analyze Swift's use of satire in the novel *Gulliver's Travels*. I argue that the satirical elements have given the work its long-lasting popularity and relevance." Then have students turn the purpose statement into a thesis or claim that sums up their argument.

Next, have students identify the evidence they will use to support their claim. This is where students' skills with using textual evidence come into play. They might use specific examples, details, evidence, and quotes from the piece of literature, and in some cases, you may want them to draw from outside sources, as well. They may need to refute other common interpretations.

This type of writing generally includes some sort of personal response that shows how the reader makes connections between the piece of literature and his own experiences and observations. Finally, have students follow the rest of the writing process as described in the earlier sections, from prewriting through drafting, revising, sharing, and proofreading.

Have students read each other's argument essays and use the following checklist to provide feedback:

- Is the claim clearly stated and adequately focused?
- Does the essay have enough support and detail? In which places could the writer provide more examples and details?
- Does the writer use transitional words and phrases to connect ideas?
- Is the introduction interesting, and does it draw the reader into the paper?
- Does the conclusion restate the claim and end the paper in a strong way? Does it make a recommendation or call to action? Does it emphasize the importance of the topic and argument?
- Is there any emotionally charged or inflammatory language that should be removed?
- Does the writer have a clear understanding of audience and purpose for the paper?
- Has the writer avoided any logical fallacies?
- Has the writer included and refuted counterclaims and opposing viewpoints?
- Can you identify any errors in spelling, punctuation, capitalization, grammar, or usage that the writer needs to correct?

## A LESSON PLAN FOR ARGUMENT WRITING

The AVID program's *The Write Path* (Crain, Mullen, & Swanson, 2002) presents a great approach and lesson plan for guiding students in writing an argument essay, noting that argument is the most common form of discourse in academic writing, requiring the reader to take a position and support it with effective use of evidence. The plan includes the following steps:

1. Begin with some instruction in logic or syllogisms to help students observe how logic works and why it is important in argument writing.
2. Provide students a variety of examples of argument and editorials.

3. Conduct a close reading of one argument as a whole class, and have students take note of claims or thesis, evidence, audience, and logical and emotional appeals used by the writer.
4. Read and study other examples independently or in small groups.
5. Brainstorm a list of issues about which students feel strongly.
6. Develop an outline or graphic organizer to plan out the essay.
7. Identify which research they will need to do and how they will find what they need.
8. Spend time on research and collaboration, and conduct minilessons on logical and emotional appeal, different forms of argument (speech, essay, letter), writing good introductions (and practicing writing different versions of an introduction), methods of organizing an argument, and developing body paragraphs.
9. Have students check for adequate evidence.
10. Write the body paragraphs first and the introduction afterward.
11. Provide peer feedback and time for revision.
12. Receive feedback on editing and conventions.
13. Conduct a read-around to share their final pieces of writing.
14. Submit the finished piece to a real audience, such as the newspaper, the principal, or some other person.

## AN OPPOSING VIEWPOINTS ARGUMENT

The Common Core writing standard for argument writing specifies that students must address counterarguments and counterclaims in their essays. This argument writing task is based on the Opposing Viewpoints database, part of the Gale databases. If you have access to this database through your school district or a local library, it is a great resource for argument writing topics. The database presents a number of different subject categories, many of them controversial in nature. It also provides sources on the topics that reflect both sides of the issue, from editorials to scholarly articles.

Because the sources provided address both sides of the issue, that is, present opposing viewpoints, students can read through a variety of articles reflecting various opinions and then determine their own positions, write their claims, and also more deliberately address counterclaims.

Opposing Viewpoints include the following general categories: "Business and Economics"; "Energy and Environmentalism"; "Health and Medicine"; "Law and Politics"; "National Debate Topics"; "Science, Technology and Ethics"; "Society and Culture"; and "War and Diplomacy." Each topic then has a huge number of subtopics.

Clicking on "View All" brings up the complete list. Each subtopic is a hyperlink that takes the student to a list of sources. The types of sources include the following: "Featured Viewpoints," "Statistics," "Images," "Reference Sources," "Biographies," "Magazines," "Audio," "News," "Academic Journals," "Websites," and "Primary Sources."

When using the Opposing Viewpoints database, you have the choice to either assign a topic to students and choose a number of readings for them to use as source material or allow students to choose their own topics and select their own sources for that topic.

Let's assume that you assign students to write an essay on global warming. You might select a number of articles and sources for students to study and take notes on in preparation for writing their essays. For the global warming topic, you might select an article called "Global Warming and Climate Change Can Be Stopped If People Try Harder," an article in support of Scott Pruitt (current EPA director) and one against Pruitt, an article titled "Climate Change Controversies" from the *Environmental Encyclopedia*, and an article called "Climate Change Is a Waste Management Issue." Be sure to select sources that reflect a range of different ideas and opinions.

One of the topics in the "Law and Politics" section is on refugees in the United States, currently a controversial issue with the influx of Syrian refugees and those from other countries. You might select the following articles: "Trump's Executive Order Is Constitutional," "Trump's Travel Restriction and Ban Create Uncertainty," "Executive Order Barring Refugees Will Not Prevent Terrorism," and "Extreme Vetting for Refugees: Already Here," as well as an article about sanctuary cities. These articles would give students a wealth of information to construct their own arguments. Follow this procedure for the Opposing Viewpoints writing task:

1. Assign a topic that students will write about, or allow students to choose one of the topics from the database. Students will need

access to laptops, Chromebooks, or a computer lab in order to access the database.

2. If assigning a topic, specify which articles you would like students to read and study. They will not have time to read all of the articles and sources provided. If choosing their own topics, students will need to select their own articles, but caution them to choose those that reflect various opinions on the topic.

3. Provide students time to read the articles and take notes. Suggestions for note taking using summary, paraphrase, and quotation are provided in chapter 7. Remind students that they need to write down all the bibliographic information for each source they use and that their note-taking system needs to make it clear which information comes from which source.

4. Following the note taking, have students choose positions on the issue and write out claim statements. You may want to work with them closely during this process and make sure that each student has a clear claim or thesis statement for the essays they will write. If you wish, you can also assign students to create an outline for their essays. Because the database includes visual and audio sources, you might consider requiring students to incorporate a visual into their essays. See recommendations for multimodal text in chapter 9.

5. Provide adequate time for drafting and revising. Conduct minilessons in addressing counterclaims, using source material, correctly citing sources, constructing a works-cited page, and so forth. If possible, conference with students about their rough drafts. Allow for peer review of the essays, as well.

6. Have students prepare final drafts of their essays. Because students' essays will reflect a variety of opinions and perspectives on their topics, provide time for them to share their papers, perhaps reading the essays in small groups, presenting a portion of their essays to the class, or having a debate or philosophical chairs activity to share ideas.

## KEY IDEAS IN THIS CHAPTER

- Students need direct instruction in strategies and techniques for writing argument essays.
- Arguments address topics of controversy and also anticipate opposing viewpoints and counterclaims.
- Common Core writing standard 1 addresses various elements of argument writing.
- Writing good arguments requires lots of prewriting and planning, such as outlining.
- When writing arguments, students need to consider audience carefully, establish their ethos or credibility, and craft an effective claim or thesis statement.
- Students may also need to gather evidence for support and carefully organize, outline, and structure their essays.
- Helping students to identify and avoid common logical fallacies is important.
- In argument writing, students need to use all the stages of the writing process, an appropriate formal tone, and good academic language and word choice.
- Using models of good argument writing is an effective way to teach argument writing.

# 7

# RESEARCH WRITING

**M**any writing assignments and performance tasks you may ask students to complete involve library and internet research. Research skills are crucial informational literacy skills that we need to help students develop. Research methodology and how to incorporate source material into one's writing are also challenging to teach and can be time consuming. With research writing assignments, students will need to go beyond their own ideas and opinions and incorporate information from outside sources.

The Common Core State Standards also place emphasis on research skills. Anchor writing standards 7 and 8 address research for writing and presenting information from multiple digital and print sources. For grades 9 and 10 students, standard 7 specifies that students will "[c]onduct short as well as more sustained research projects to answer a question (including a self-generated question) or solve a problem; narrow or broaden the inquiry when appropriate; synthesize multiple sources on the subject, demonstrating an understanding of the subject under investigation" (Council of Chief State School Officers and National Governors Association, 2010). This standard highlights several key research skills, including narrowing a topic and synthesizing information from various sources.

Writing standard 8 for grades 9 and 10 states that students will "[g]ather relevant information from multiple authoritative print and digital sources, using advanced searches effectively; assess the usefulness of each source in answering the research question; integrate information into the text selectively to maintain the flow of ideas, avoiding plagiarism and following a standard format for citation" (Council of Chief State School Officers and National Governors Association, 2010). Several key research skills are present in this standard as well: selecting and evaluating sources, using search engines, taking notes, integrating source material, avoiding plagiarism, and citing sources. This chapter includes some strategies and ideas to help students build these skills.

With some assignments, you may provide students with a number of sources from which to select material; in other, more open-ended assignments, you may ask them to do their own source searches and choose appropriate material for their topics. A research paper or report often has a primarily informative purpose, although students may make an argument related to the topic as well. Follow the steps and suggestions in this chapter when asking students to complete a research paper of any kind.

## PLANNING AND PREWRITING

Students will need to begin by finding a topic, unless you have assigned particular topics to students. In most cases, students begin with topics that are too broad, and they will need to narrow the topic; however, they may need to do a bit of preliminary research in order to identify a sufficiently narrowed topic. Reviewing a general source, such as an encyclopedia article or Wikipedia entry, is a good place to start narrowing a topic.

Next, have them write a research question, one that has an open-ended answer. Have students begin by identifying a general topic they are interested in. For example, if they want to write about some aspect of technology, then they will need to narrow it down considerably, perhaps settling on a topic like video games. Their question needs to be one that will require some exploration. After doing some preliminary reading, ask students to narrow their topics down and then write a thesis statement. Do a brainstorming activity, such as the one in Figure 7.1, to help them generate some questions and settle on a thesis statement:

The next step for students is to begin locating and evaluating possible sources. You may want to specify a minimum number of sources

| General topic: _____ | | | | |
|---|---|---|---|---|
| Narrowed topic: _____ | | | | |
| Who? | What? What happened? | When? | Where? | Why? How? |
| | | | | |
| | | | | |
| | | | | |
| | | | | |
| | | | | |
| | | | | |
| Research Question: _____ _____ | | | | |
| Thesis Statement: _____ _____ _____ | | | | |

**Figure 7.1.   Brainstorming activity**

students are required to use. For shorter writing assignments, you might specify three sources and for larger papers as many as ten. It might be useful to conduct a minilesson to illustrate for students the difference between primary and secondary sources, as well as providing students with some tips for doing advanced internet searches.

Teach students how to use the databases your school district subscribes to. These databases will be by far the most useful sources of information on most topics. Steer students away from doing basic Google searches using only general terms because the results provided are generally not useful. In the beginning stages, students may want to do some preliminary reading in general encyclopedias or online to get an overview of the topic. Then they can begin searching for more substantive source material.

Have students use notecards to write down the bibliographical information for all of the sources they decide to use in their papers. Their sources may include books; magazine and newspaper articles; journal articles and other sources from databases; government documents; other types of documents; videos and multimedia sources; and even such primary sources as interviews, speeches, autobiographies, and firsthand accounts. The types of sources used will depend greatly on the topic.

The next step is to teach students some skills involved in evaluating the credibility and usefulness of their sources. The advantage of using academic databases is that the quality of the information and material found there is better because they are scholarly materials from reputable publications. This is also true of more specialized search engines, such as Google Scholar (https://scholar.google.com).

Also, for general websites, teach students about the different domain names: .com, .net, .edu, .gov, and so forth. A general principle for research is to prefer sources that are not .com sites, although again, that may depend on the particular topic. In general, ask students to consider three factors to assess the usefulness and credibility of their sources:

1. **Relevance:** Is the source relevant to my topic and helpful in answering my research question. Does it have good, accurate content?
2. **Accuracy:** Can it be verified by more than one source? Is it up to date? What are the author's qualifications and credentials?
3. **Objectivity:** Does it present or acknowledge multiple viewpoints on the topic? Is it biased in some way? Who sponsored or wrote the information?

Students must be especially cautious of information from the web. Remind students—many of whom tend to assume that, if they find something online, then it is automatically true—that anyone can create a website and that there is no "internet police" to monitor the content or make sure the information is valid. Also, tell students that, if they cannot identify the author or sponsor of the site, then they should not use it as a source. Of course, students also need to determine if the site and its content are useful for their purposes. Use the following types of questions to evaluate websites they are considering using.

—⟨⟨⟨⟩⟩⟩—

### Evaluating a Website

1. What is the name and author or sponsoring organization of the website?
2. What is the URL (web address) of the site?
3. What is the author's or institution's credibility on the topic—their expertise or authority?
4. What is the purpose of the site: to sell something, to promote a political agenda, to provide information, to make an argument? Are there any signs of biased information?
5. Is the information current and up to date? When was it posted online or last updated?
6. Does the site include a bibliography or list of sources on which the content is based?
7. Does the source provide information that is useful for my topic? If so, what will I use this source for?

—⟨⟨⟨⟩⟩⟩—

## TAKING NOTES AND AVOIDING PLAGIARISM

Begin by making sure that students have written down the bibliographic information for each source on a separate notecard. These should contain all the information students will need to cite the source correctly in their works-cited pages. If you have access to electronic note-taking and research software, that would be the preferable choice.

For books, students must have the complete title, the author, the name of the publisher, and the copyright date. If the source is a website, then the card should list the name of the website, the name of the specific web page used, the author or sponsoring institution, the web address, the date last updated or posted, and the date the information was accessed.

For their note taking, have students make a separate notecard or an electronic file for every single note they take from their sources, making sure that they have a clear system for indicating which information comes from which source. Some teachers recommend handwriting notecards for this part of the process because it helps students avoid copying and pasting information from websites and unintentionally plagiarizing. The notes that students take may be in one of the following formats:

1. **Direct quotation:** This contains exact wording from the original source. Be sure to include quotation marks so that you know it is a direct quote. Also, you must include the page or paragraph number where the quote comes from. Only take quotation notes for those sections you are sure you want to quote word for word.

2. **Summary:** This is usually a brief statement of the main ideas. It is a more condensed version of the material. It is sometimes useful to take summary notes when you are just looking for main ideas. A summary might mean summarizing the main idea of a passage with three or four paragraphs, or even a whole article, in one or two sentences.

3. **Paraphrase:** This is a restatement of the original ideas in your own words. Be very careful to accurately paraphrase so that you are not unintentionally plagiarizing from your source. Go through the original passage, pick out one idea at a time, and then state each idea in your own words. The paraphrase will probably be about the same length as the original or maybe slightly longer.

In some cases, students' notes may contain a combination of both paraphrase and quotation, where only a portion of the original is exact wording from the source.

It is important to make sure students understand what plagiarism is: the intentional or unintentional use of an author's words or ideas without giving credit to the original source. It is unacceptable and grounds for failure because it is dishonest and a form of cheating. It is taking credit for someone else's words or ideas and presenting them as if they were your own. Careful note taking will help students prevent plagiarism, which is why it is important to guide them carefully through the note-taking process and check their notes to make sure they are not plagiarizing.

Remind students also that these rules refer to all source material, including digital and online sources. Carefully writing down all the bibliographic information for all sources will also help students to prepare their works-cited pages, which provide the publication information for all sources used in the paper. Present minilessons in how to use the common citation makers, such as EasyBib (www.easybib.com), and make sure they know how to use the citation tools that the databases provide.

It might be helpful to refer to the many valuable resources available on the Purdue University Online Writing Lab (OWL) website (https:// owl.english.purdue.edu/owl). The Purdue OWL includes materials on all the following: research and citation methods for both MLA and APA styles, formatting and style guides, directions for in-text (parenthetical) citations and works-cited-page entries, and a sample student paper and works-cited page in MLA style. There is also a PowerPoint for MLA style that you can use in class.

For all database sources, a "cite" link is available that gives the correct citation for whichever citation format is being used. This makes it easy for students to copy and paste that citation into their works-cited page, although it is important for them to always check to make sure it is correct. The online databases are now updated to the new eighth edition of MLA.

## SYNTHESIZING INFORMATION FROM DIFFERENT SOURCES

As students begin writing their papers, they will need to synthesize information from different sources. Students should use the source material they have gathered during note taking wherever it is useful to support their ideas in their papers. Remind students that a good portion of their papers should be written in their own words, but they will also be frequently adding information and evidence from their sources. Synthesizing requires blending the writer's words with the source material.

It may also require blending information from one of your sources with another source.

All included quotations should be integrated into the writer's sentences. Give students some practice with introducing quotations so that they do not just stick quotes into their papers with no connection to the surrounding sentences. These are often referred to as hanging quotes or quote bombs. Teach them to use such introductory phrases as "According to the article," "A recent articles states that," and "The study by Jones reveals that."

Provide students with a good list of verbs to introduce source material so that they do not use *said* or *stated* over and over: *acknowledges, demonstrates, implies, suggests, offers, responds, speculates, argues, contends, asserts, believes, compares, confirms, maintains, questions, reports, observes, shows,* and *writes*. Have your class read some sample research papers, while drawing their attention to the way that the writers incorporate their source material. Most writing handbooks and textbooks, as well as online sources, include some sample student papers that you can read and review with students.

## ORGANIZING THE PAPER

The organizational strategies for a research paper are no different from those for any other type of essay or paper, except that the research paper is probably longer and incorporates more source material. After students have completed their research and note taking, require them to prepare an outline for their papers, which they can follow while they are writing. If students have done their note taking on notecards, then this process becomes much easier because they can organize their notecards into categories, which become the major subtopics and parts of the paper.

Have students start with writing a good introduction that states their thesis statement. This is a good time to ask them to reassess their thesis statements and be sure that they match the content of their papers and that the source material supports the thesis.

The body and content of the paper should relate to the controlling idea of the paper. During the organizational process, students will want to think about which organizational structure to use. The structure will depend largely on the topic. They may choose a chronological order for some topics or an emphatic order, in which the most compelling evidence is placed first in the paper, from strongest to weakest. Some topics will lend themselves to a cause-effect structure or comparison-contrast.

Encourage students to think about incorporating visuals into their papers, as well, such as tables, charts, graphs, illustrations, photographs, maps, and so forth. Teach them to label and title any visuals they include, and remind them that information in visual form also needs to be cited, just like any other source material (see further suggestions for multimodal text in chapter 9).

## DRAFTING THE PAPER

For the actual writing of the paper, follow the same steps and procedures you would with any other type of writing. Because research papers are usually longer, it may take more class time, however. Students should begin by chunking their information into categories, following their outlines. Encourage them to write a topic sentence for each paragraph or section in the paper, so that each section presents a topic sentence that supports the thesis, followed by support for that specific topic.

Quoted, paraphrased, and summarized information must be integrated and introduced into the paper. Use transitional words to introduce all quotes and ideas from your sources. Make sure that, as they are writing, students do not begin to merely dump information into their papers. Their papers should not merely report information but should be a research-based argument. This requires using the source material purposefully, not just sticking it into their papers. If students introduce and explain their source material, showing the reader how it relates to the main ideas and the thesis, then they will have written a successful research paper.

Give students some time to read through drafts of their papers in small peer-response groups. This will help them get feedback and suggestions for improving their papers and also provide a chance to observe what other writers are doing successfully in their own papers.

## REVISING THE PAPER

Before students complete their final research papers, have them spend time focusing on revision of all three parts: introduction, body, and conclusion. Like any paper, the introduction should draw the reader into the essay, explain why the topic is an interesting and important one, and clearly state the thesis. Have students try writing a couple different versions of their introductions to determine which one they think is the best.

In revising the body, students will want to focus largely on their use of evidence and source material, making sure that information from sources is adequately incorporated and cited correctly. They should also make sure that they have transitions between the parts of the paper.

Finally, the paper should end with a strong conclusion that sums up the thesis and evidence presented. If the paper is focused on a particular problem, then they may want to state a possible solution and its benefits or make a recommendation. Have students use the following checklist to revise their papers:

- Is my purpose and thesis clearly stated in the introduction?
- Does my paper fit the requirements of the assignment?
- Have I used a blend of summary, paraphrase, and direct quotes, and have I cited all the source material in the paper?
- Have I followed the correct format for MLA papers (or Chicago or APA) and included a works-cited or references page in correct form?
- Have I fully developed the paper with lots of relevant evidence?
- Are there any details that do not relate to my topic and purpose and should be deleted?
- Where should I add additional details or more explanation?
- Is my paper interesting to read? Are my tone and style appropriate for the topic and purpose?
- Have I provided a strong conclusion that sums up my paper and thesis?
- Have I provided connections and transitions between the parts of the paper?
- Are there any errors in sentence structure, spelling, capitalization, punctuation, or grammar that I need to correct?

## USING MULTIMEDIA TO PREPARE A RESEARCH REPORT

Because research papers tend to take a lot of time for students to write, it is always a good idea to give them an opportunity to share the results of their research with the class. Consider requiring students to give a multimedia presentation of their research papers. Assuming that you have enough electronic equipment available in your classroom, this activity provides an excellent way to help students learn more about multimedia resources and how to use them.

The choice of media and software may depend on the equipment and software available in your classroom, but generally, if you have internet access and a projector that connects to a computer or laptop, then students will be able to construct a high-quality multimedia presentation.

Ask students to prepare an outline that gives an overview of the content of the research project and clearly presents the thesis. Then ask them to locate several pieces of media they can also incorporate into their presentations. These might include video, audiotapes, podcasts, graphics, photographs, PowerPoint or Prezi presentations, movie clips, sound recordings, music, artwork, and other graphic elements.

It is possible that your students will know a lot more about these resources and how to use them than you do. As they should do with any source material, have students evaluate the multimedia they are planning to use to make sure they are credible and accurate. They should plan to incorporate at least three forms of audio, video, or graphic images throughout their presentations.

Remind students also that a presentation requires carefully planning and practicing it with several run-throughs ahead of time. They should also make sure that the available equipment is adequate for their specific forms of multimedia. (See more suggestions for multimodal text in chapter 9.)

The final portion of this chapter includes sample research assignments that are successful for generating good research writing.

## VIEWPOINTS ESSAY

Although this project was used with college-bound writing students (high school seniors), it could easily be adapted for many different grade levels and content areas. The project requires having students choose groups by topic (or assigning students to a group). The assignment has two parts: a written research essay and a group presentation to the class. I used topics that come from Dorothy U. Seyler's writing textbook *Read, Reason, Write: An Argument Text and Reader* (2012). Students were asked to choose one of the following topics and form groups for that topic: media, the internet and social media, the environment, sports talk and sports battles, marriage and gender, education, censorship and free speech, and ethics.

The following is the assignment sheet that students were provided. Students were provided with several readings focusing on specific aspects for each of the topics. For example, if students chose the sports talk topic, then they read several articles related to paying college athletes, women's athletics, and performance enhancing drugs.

—◦◦◦—

### Viewpoints Essay Assignment

This assignment has two parts: a written essay and a presentation to the class. Follow the procedure below:

1. Choose one of the topics: media, environment, sports, censorship, ethics, or marriage and gender. Readings for each topic will be provided. Form groups by topic.
2. Read, annotate, and study all the assigned readings to get a sense of the overall topic and the different factors and viewpoints involved.
3. Prepare a group presentation for the class on the given topic. The presentation should be ten to fifteen minutes in length. It should include an overview of the topic, a summary or review of several or all of the different essays included in the readings, and a discussion of the argument you plan to make in your own paper. You are also required to incorporate visuals or multimedia as part of your presentation. Audience discussion and activities are also recommended.

4. Your group will give your presentation to the class on the day you are assigned.

5. The written essay is an individual project. Choose a specific, narrowed aspect of your topic that you want to write your essay about. The essay is *not* a summary of the topic or the different readings but should present your own research argument on the topic. You will decide what your argument will be after reading through the material on the topic. For example, if you choose ethics, you might choose to write an argument about the US government's use of torture following 9/11.

6. The viewpoints essay should be approximately four pages long and is due on the day specified.

Those who chose the education topic read articles about the relationship between exercise and learning, college preparation, standardized testing, and technology and education. Students used these articles to develop a claim for their own argument essays on the topic. They were also expected to cite them as sources in their essays. This particular project did not require them to use additional outside sources, but they were given the option to do so if they wished.

You can always adapt the requirements and length of the viewpoints papers according to the ability levels and needs of your specific students. A rubric was also created to fairly and effectively evaluate each group's final presentation to the class (Table 7.1).

## THE I-SEARCH PAPER

The I-Search paper is a specific type of research project designed by Macrorie (1998). It is an inquiry-based project that mirrors real-world writing when we do research in order to find the answer to a particular question. For the I-Search paper, students self-select their questions, think carefully about the research process they use, and draw meaningful conclusions at the end of the process.

The I-Search requires teachers to set some clear requirements for the project, and it usually has a limited focus. Students choose a topic that is meaningful to them and brainstorm questions they have about it.

**Table 7.1.   Viewpoints presentation rubric**

| | 25: Excellent | 20: Good | 15: Needs Improvement | 10: Poor |
|---|---|---|---|---|
| **Delivery** | Direct eye contact | Some direct eye contact | Minimal eye contact | No eye contact with audience |
| | Some use of notes and resources | Adequate volume and inflection by some group members | Mostly reading from notes | Entire presentation read from notes |
| | Good, clear voice | Occasional use of *like* or *you know* | Uneven volume with little inflection | All group members speak in monotone |
| | Good pace and delivery by all group members | | Frequent stumbling and use of *like* and *you know* | Repetitive use of *like, you know*, and other fillers |
| | Little use of *like* and *you know* as filler | | | |
| **Content** | All group members demonstrate thorough and detailed understanding of the topic and readings | All group members demonstrate good understanding of topic and readings | Most group members demonstrate good understanding of topic and readings | Most group members demonstrate little understanding of topic and readings or complexity of issues |
| | All recognize complexity of topic | Some awareness of complexity of the topic | Lack of awareness of range of issues and complexity | Little use of specific details and examples |
| | Provides clear and specific details and examples | Provides a few clear and specific details | Only occasional use of specific details | No excerpts or examples from readings |
| | Use of excerpts from readings | Some excerpts from readings included | Very few excerpts from readings | |

| | 25: Excellent | 20: Good | 15: Needs Improvement | 10: Poor |
|---|---|---|---|---|
| **Organization** | Well organized and thoroughly prepared participation on the part of all group members | Generally good organization of the presentation | Somewhat disorganized presentation and lack of preparation by some group members | Poor organization of presentation |
| | | Evidence of adequate planning | | Group members frequently unsure how to proceed |
| **Enthusiasm and Audience Engagement** | Some audience involvement | Some audience involvement | Little audience involvement included | No audience involvement; lecture only |
| | Group members demonstrate enthusiasm about topic | Group members demonstrate some enthusiasm | Little enthusiasm demonstrated by group members | Lack of enthusiasm by most members of the group |
| | Convinces audience to recognize the importance of the subject | Raises audience awareness of the topic to some degree | Raises audience awareness about a few aspects of the topic | Group shows no interest in the topic presented |
| | | | | Fails to interest audience in the topic |
| **Appropriate Length** | Ten minutes or more | Seven to ten minutes | Approximately five minutes | Less than five minutes |

Next, they select a central question that will become the focus of their inquiry and help them identify possible sources. Generally, there are three parts included in the final paper: the research question, the search process, and findings. Some teachers vary these parts to include the search story, search results, and search reflections.

The following I-Search project was designed in collaboration with colleague Matthew Isom for our sophomore American literature students. Students were studying the concept of modernism, and the project goal was to meet Common Core standard 7 as well as expand their knowledge of the concept of modernism and how it related to the literature students were studying in class. We began the project by asking students to read a lengthy encyclopedia article on modernism from *World Book Encyclopedia*, available through the school databases. We provided them with a list of possible topics and then presented the following assignment sheet.

———◦∂∕◦———

### I-Search Paper on Modernism

## Standards Addressed

W.7: Conduct short as well as more sustained research projects to answer a question (including a self-generated question) or solve a problem; narrow or broaden the inquiry when appropriate; synthesize multiple sources on the subject, demonstrating understanding of the subject under investigation.

## Overview

The I-Search paper is a research and writing project that will demonstrate your ability to generate a research question, locate sources, interpret the meaning of what you find, organize your thoughts, analyze and evaluate your findings, and draw conclusions about your topic. In addition, you will need to effectively write to communicate what you have learned. The I-Search paper shares with the reader the history of your paper and explains the process you followed in conducting the research. It is a reflective document that asks you to think about what you learned from the experience.

## Requirements of the Project

1. The paper must have four parts:

- My research question
- My search process
- What I learned (findings)
- Works-cited page

The first three parts must be labeled with section headings in your paper. The works-cited page is always labeled "Works Cited."

2. The paper should be four to five typed, double-spaced pages. Use no larger than twelve-point font and no wider than one-inch margins.

3. The paper must use sources from the library databases; books; articles from newspapers, magazines, or journals; other printed material; and websites. You must have at least four sources. You are not allowed to use Wikipedia as a source. Be sure to use quotation marks for any direct wording taken from sources, and integrate the quotes into your sentences (and be sure to cite the source).

4. The paper must have a works-cited page in MLA format that includes all the sources you referred to in the paper. Use a writer's handbook, Citation Machine (http://citationmachine.net), or EasyBib (www.easybib.com) to help you format the works-cited page correctly.

Here is a detailed explanation of each of the three parts of the paper:

## Part I: My Research Question

Start by identifying your general topic and the research question that you want to explore. Refer to the encyclopedia article on modernism and the attached list of sample topics. You may choose one of these topics, but you still have to come up with your own research question about the topic. Choose something that you are curious about. In this section of the paper, which can be written before you have done very much research, you should describe what you already know about the topic (prior knowledge), why you are interested in it, and which question or questions you would like to answer. Use these questions to guide you:

- Why have I chosen this topic?
- What do I already know about this topic?
- What questions do I have?
- What research question do I really want to focus on?
- What do I hope to discover in order to answer the research question?

Use coherent paragraphs for this section (two to three); do not just write a list of answers to the questions.

## Part 2: My Search Process

In this section, you will describe the process you used to search for information on your topic. Take notes and keep a learning log of your work as you go in order to be prepared to write this section. Discuss which sources you started with, how helpful and reliable they were, new questions that came up as you searched, what you had trouble finding, and frustrations you encountered along the way. Be specific about explaining your research methods, and talk about how useful some of your specific sources were. Here are some sentence starters to use:

- When I searched the databases, I found . . .
- On the internet, I found a few articles that . . .
- After doing some research, I realized. . .
- I was finally able to find . . .
- I was frustrated because I had trouble finding . . .
- I was never able to find . . .

## Part 3: What I Learned (My Findings)

This section allows you to focus on what you have learned as a result of completing your research project. It should include the specific information you found about your topic and should be the longest section of the paper. Be sure to use summary, paraphrase, or quotations to incorporate the information into your paper, and be sure to specify the source of all information.

Note: Any time you use actual wording from a source, it must be in quotation marks and must be cited so that the reader knows they are not your words and so readers can identify which source the quote comes from. Use introductory phrases such as "According to Samuelson" and "Robert P. Smith, in his article [fill in the blank], states." Always refer to authors by their last names. Part 3 should be several paragraphs long and must include the following:

- A summary of your findings and conclusions. This section should provide the "answer" to the research question you started with. Make sure the information you include is logically related to the research question you posed earlier.
- Reflection on your topic. It explains what you have learned from this project and what it means to you.
- A modernist works of literature that we have read this semester. Discuss how your findings relate to the particular work. How do your research findings affect your understanding of the work? How has the work affected your thinking on your topic?
- How has your research affected your thinking about the nature of the modern world and modern life?

Finally, include your works-cited page on a separate page in correct MLA format.

The following is the list of topics related to modernism that we brainstormed and allowed students to choose from:

- Modernist attitudes
- Philosophy of Nietzsche
- Existentialism
- Spectator sports
- Babe Ruth
- Technology
- Radio
- Cinema
- Red Scare (1920s or 1950s)
- Palmer Raids
- Prejudice in the 1920s
- World War I
- World War II
- Rebuilding of Europe
- Baseball
- Prohibition/Volstead Act
- Women's movement/suffrage
- President Herbert Hoover

- President Franklin Delano Roosevelt
- Harlem Renaissance
- Child labor
- Flappers
- Credit and debt
- President Warren G. Harding
- President Calvin Coolidge
- President Harry Truman
- Marxism
- Feminism
- Al Capone
- The mob/gangsters
- Charles Lindbergh
- Jazz music
- Music in the 1920s/1930s
- Dance in the 1920s
- Bootlegging
- Speakeasies
- Scopes "Monkey" Trial
- Immigration
- The Fitzgeralds, Scott and Zelda
- The Great Migration
- Industry/manufacturing
- Industrialism
- The automobile
- The press/newspapers
- Expatriates/Lost Generation
- Sinclair Lewis
- Ernest Hemingway
- Art in the 1920s
- Prosperity
- Opulence
- Stock market crash
- Great Depression
- Sigmund Freud
- Carl Jung
- Cubism
- Imagism

- Surrealism
- Dadaism
- Fascism
- Postimpressionism
- Baudelaire
- Flaubert
- Avant-garde
- Einstein: theory of relativity
- Abstract expressionism
- Marcel Proust
- Capitalism
- Atonal music
- Stravinsky
- Schoenberg
- Realism
- Naturalism
- Regionalism
- Assembly line/factory model
- Aviation
- Architecture
- The telephone
- Spirit of rebellion/individualism
- Urbanization
- Russian Revolution/Lenin
- Nineteenth Amendment
- Atomic bomb
- The New Deal
- Isolationism
- Disillusionment
- Hemingway code hero
- Stream of consciousness
- The Dust Bowl

This project gave us a great deal of insight into students' research skills and processes and also insight into the struggles they encountered with search engines and source materials. Because students were required to make a connection between their topics and a piece of modernist literature we had read, it allowed them to demonstrate their ability to apply the concepts they had learned about their topics and draw conclusions about the broader impact of modernism.

You may also want to locate or design a rubric that you can use for scoring of the I-Search papers. We evaluated the papers in the following categories: introduction and research question, the search, the results, discussion and application of ideas, use of source material, and correctness.

Many of my students wrote excellent I-Search papers. The following example by Nicholas is a good paper, although you may notice he cites too few sources and could have further developed the "What I Learned" section of his paper. Nicholas's paper as reprinted here does not include his works-cited page.

—◦◦◦—

## My Research Question: How Ethical Were Businessmen of the 1900s?

I chose this topic because I have a little prior knowledge about business of the early twentieth century but still a general sense of obscurity toward the time period. Obviously, some businessmen engaged in illegal dealings. However, were these actions commonplace? For example, did many men on Wall Street engage in nefarious stock trading? I hope to seek an answer through my research of prominent businessmen. I want to focus on the question, "How ethical were the practices of the top businessmen of the 1900s?" I want to discover whether the most remembered men of the early 1900s came by their wealth honestly or if their business practices were somewhat shady.

I know that many men of the time period were somewhat nefarious in their actions. From my Spanish class, I found out that Cornelius Vanderbilt financed a war against an American who was ruling in Nicaragua. While this isn't exactly business related (although some may argue that the American, Wagner, was interfering with Vanderbilt's operations and therefore his actions were business related), it is an example of an extreme length that some men went to. Additionally, I know from my Twentieth-Century History class that the most powerful men of the early 1900s were labeled "robber barons." However, there were those, such as Henry Ford, who paid their workers decent wages and benefited the community. Due to inconsistencies such as these, I decided to investigate further into the business affairs of men of the time.

In order to do this, I hope to discover many aspects of business from a century ago. One of my main questions is whether illegal dealings were commonplace. If they were, I am also interested in whether illegal actions were a requirement for success. Could a man rise to the top of an industry and stay there, all while staying within the law? These questions will help me answer my main research question: How ethical were businessmen of the 1900s? Though it sounds vague, illegal proceedings are commonly documented, especially if caught. Therefore, any objective data (or a lack thereof) that I come across will also assist me in directly determining an answer to my question. I hope to discover some hard evidence toward illegal business dealings of the time period, which will easily ratify the question I ask. In order to complete this task, I plan on focusing on the most successful men of the time, for two main reasons. The first is that I will determine whether the most successful men had to engage in illegal acts to keep their power. The answer to that will be most telling, as it will inform me about how the American economy worked as a whole during the time period. The second reason is that, as popular, renowned figures, these men will have earned large recognition in the scholastic world, and as a result, I will have lots of information to take advantage of.

## My Search Process

In order to begin searching, I first looked to online resources. I quickly identified online resources as fantastic tools. As one who has easy internet access at home, I knew that I would be able to refer back to any online sources I found with relative ease. In order to do this, I first investigated my topic and subtopics with search engines. Popular resources, such as Wikipedia, had many citations on my topic, and I would check sources that had been cited on Wikipedia when I encountered related ideas on this particular source. Additionally, my institution of learning offers access to online research databases, such as GALE and OSLIS. I used both in my research process because both are intended to be used for research papers. However, I did struggle when using the two. Because they are paid services, GALE and OSLIS both require passwords to be accessed. However, I circumvented this by speaking with a school official. Through this meeting, I received the necessary login information and was able to continue with my research. I also utilized both resources.

The Salem Public Library contains thousands of volumes of books, and I found four that were particularly useful in relation to my research topic. These four volumes are:

- *Masters of Enterprise*, by H. W. Brands
- *The Tycoons*, by Charles R. Morris
- *Giants of Enterprise*, by Richard S. Tedlow
- *In Their Time*, by Anthony J. Mayo and Nitin Nohria

These four books increased my knowledge of my topic greatly. Although they were printed ten years ago, not much of our understanding of the early 1900s has changed, so these books were still very helpful. Having paper sources was a large benefit to my research because I could read them on the go. As one who does not have a smartphone, my internet resources were not always available.

When I did my research, I was slightly disappointed with the information I found. Really, my results should have been expected, considering that I had narrowed down my topic to America's wealthiest businessmen. The sources that I found were mostly biographies on such men as Andrew Carnegie, Jay Gould, John Rockefeller, and Cornelius Vanderbilt. As a result, while I did discover some illegal business tactics, the majority of the information I received on illegal procedures was circumstantial to each man. I struggled with locating information on industry standards; for example, I know that in the 1980s it was common to manipulate the price of stocks. This type of information about industries was more difficult to find than what I had found in biographies, and so I widened my search parameters to incorporate it. I did this by searching for keywords that were slightly vaguer, such as "business tactics."

## What I Learned

I discovered much of what I was attempting to learn. In the first place, the biographies I used eventually gave me enough information on my topic. I was taught by these biographies to make interpretations about the business leaders of the age. For example, I had to interpret what I was reading and understand that price cutting is unethical. As I was engaged by my sources, I believe my capabilities as a researcher expanded due to my intense search. Furthermore, I grew my knowledge and discovered that the businessmen of the 1900s were not ethical.

First and foremost, these businessmen padded their investments by creating trusts. A trust is a large corporation consisting of several, smaller corporations, which, when joined, monopolize an industry or market. Trusts were formally banned in 1890 with the passage of the Sherman Antitrust Act, but trusts still formed. For example, when the Standard Oil trust of John D. Rockefeller was dissolved by the Sherman Act in 1892, Rockefeller just re-created the trust and ran it for another twenty years (Brands 92). J. P. Morgan, a famous banker, created the Northern Securities Corporation (a trust) to dominate the northwestern railroads and was eventually prosecuted for it (Morris 236). There were trusts in just about every industry imaginable; tobacco, steel, oil, tin, transportation, and even sugar all had trusts dominating the majority of market share. Over a period of ten years (1895–1904), 1,800 companies disappeared through mergers and consolidations, proving that there was a growing trend to form trusts (Morris 252). Due to the high amount of trusts, I can tell that there was certainly a lot of unethical regulation of trade in this time period.

In addition to this, another common activity was undercutting. Undercutting is the act of selling a product or service at a lower price than a competitor would. Often, competitors would lower their prices to match, only to find that the competing price was lowered as soon as they did. This was seen when Cornelius Vanderbilt started his transportation business. Vanderbilt ran both ferry and railroad lines and used undercutting as a main form of gaining market share (Brands 18). Rockefeller used the same tactics in securing more oil interests. In an attempt to grow Standard Oil, Rockefeller would slash his prices in those areas that he was in direct competition with (Brands 89). Andrew Carnegie followed suit with these tycoons. At one point, Carnegie literally offered to produce steel for the lowest price that the contract director could find in a competitor (Brands 59). The process of undercutting is unethical and is now regulated by the government in order to protect small businesses against large corporations.

Beyond these unethical dealings, these corporation heads often engaged in flat-out illegal activities. For example, Jay Gould and Jim Fisk created a gold corner (labeled that because they "cornered" the market) to control the price of gold (Morris 70). These two men would also later print stock certificates in a basement, dumping the stock on the market and driving the price of gold down (Morris 68).

Such illegal dealings bring to mind the character of Gatsby from *The Great Gatsby*. Gatsby was involved in illegal trade, and while the men mentioned all sold their goods legitimately, they committed illegal acts in order to do so. Discovering this radically modified my view on these historical figures. As some of the wealthiest men to have ever lived, the tycoons of the twentieth century are often idolized. However, when I discovered that they were successful mainly by cheating others, I realized that their accomplishments weren't so impressive.

## KEY IDEAS IN THIS CHAPTER

- Research skills are important information literacy skills.
- Common Core standards 7 and 8 address researching to create and present knowledge.
- Research skills include selecting and evaluating sources, using search engines, taking notes, integrating and synthesizing source material, avoiding plagiarism, and citing sources.
- In research writing, students need to find a sufficiently narrowed topic and write a research question.
- Students must learn strategies for evaluating the credibility and usefulness of their sources, especially web sources.
- Bibliographic information for sources must be carefully recorded to prevent plagiarism.
- Students must learn to do careful note taking in the form of paraphrases, summaries, and direct quotations in order to plan for writing and prevent plagiarism.
- Students should use all the stages of the writing process to draft their research papers.

- Students can share the results of their research with the audience using various forms of multimedia.
- The viewpoints essay and the I-Search paper are useful research writing projects.

# 8

# TIMED AND ON-DEMAND WRITING

One of the types of writing that students are commonly expected to do, both in high school and in college, is timed or on-demand writing tasks. As ELA teachers, we can help students to prepare for this challenging and commonly high-stakes form of writing. Many of the other writing skills students have developed will assist them in preparing for on-demand writing tasks, and the more comfortable and confident they are with their writing in general, the better they will perform in timed or on-demand writing tasks. For this reason, giving them multiple opportunities to practice is beneficial.

Some common forms of on-demand writing students are expected to complete include state assessment tests, where students are required to write an essay. Often, this test is required for high school graduation. Also, various forms of standardized tests include on-demand writing, including the SAT, Advanced Placement tests, and IB tests. Gallagher (2006) also notes that "many employers are now asking for writing samples as a part of the interview process. Why? Because they are finding huge writing deficiencies in their workforce" (p. 41). While most of us work better without the pressure of being under the clock, the reality is that students will often have to write under pressure, in academic contexts and in the real world.

Critique of standardized testing is common among teachers, and many of these points apply to standardized writing tests as well. Gardner (2008) notes that standardized writing tests are the "antithesis of effective writing assignments" (p. 67), in that students are not given any choice, little scaffolding is provided, and the usual writing process that we may teach students is ignored. Therefore, students often produce weaker writing. Although standardized writing tasks are not ideal writing situations, the fact is that students will be expected to complete a number of these types of timed, on-demand, and often high-stakes writing tasks during their academic career.

There are many things that we can and should do to help prepare students for on-demand writing. Gallagher (2006) notes that on-demand writing has become a "gate-keeping issue. Students taught to write well have the key to unlock gates to better opportunities. Students who do not write well on demand risk being locked out" (p. 41). This reason alone is rationale enough for ELA teachers to spend some time focusing on on-demand writing.

But there are other reasons we should spend time teaching timed and on-demand writing in our curriculum. Gallagher (2006) points out that students spend only 15 percent of their time in school actually writing, that on-demand writing tasks are often mandated and high-stakes, and that frequent on-demand writing will make students more comfortable with writing and build their fluency, thus better preparing them for timed writing tasks.

There are several things that students need to know to prepare for high-stakes writing tests. They include the following:

- They need to know how to understand and analyze the prompt.
- They need to have some strategies for generating ideas and organizing before they start writing, as well as revising strategies after writing.
- They need to know how their writing will be evaluated and scored. This includes an understanding of the traits that will be used to assess the writing.
- They need to have studied and examined some models for the types of essays they will be expected to write. Most states that require a writing test provide sample student papers, sometimes with scores and discussion of the rationale for the scores on the papers. Most importantly, students need to know what a passing paper looks like and understand which qualities and characteristics make a paper passing or not passing. Asking students to read and examine a sample essay with low scores, one with passing

scores, and one with exemplary scores is an effective way to help them understand the kind of essay they will need to produce.

- They need to be able to call on a variety of writing strategies that will be useful to them in on-demand or timed writing situations. Many of these are skills and strategies discussed in earlier chapters. They may include how to brainstorm, draft, revise, and edit. Have students been provided opportunities to write to a specific prompt? Have students been taught some revision strategies, such as adding details, improving word choice, using a variety of sentence structures, and editing for conventions?

Gardner (2008) recommends three approaches to timed writing tasks:

1. **Defining the task:** Even though we don't know ahead of time the exact prompt students will be writing about, we can help our students learn more about the test by using sample prompts, essays, and rubrics in our classrooms. Also, students have most likely had previous experience with timed writing, such as in-class essays, essay tests, and short-answer questions. We can use their understanding of these experiences as prior knowledge by having them focus on common composing strategies.
2. **Scaffolding the process:** This involves helping students understand how they write under pressure by reflecting on times they have had to write quickly in class and which strategies they used during timed writing. We can focus on the different processes required for timed writing and standardized tests, helping students understand the range of options they have.
3. **Exploring the task and expectations:** This involves focusing directly "on the task and the expectations for students' work—beginning by unpacking the meaning behind the prompts on standardized tests. Learning to read the writing prompts on these tests is essential to success" (p. 69).

One strategy that we can use in the classroom is to have students, especially juniors and seniors, write practice essays for writing tests. For example, a quick Google search will produce sample and previous SAT essay topics. One site that includes sample SAT writing prompts is College Board (http://collegereadiness.collegeboard.org).

Gardner (2008) recommends not using these practice tests as timed writing but instead allowing time for prewriting, drafting, collaboration, and revision so that students can better explore and practice how to approach the task when they are in the real timed writing situation. Gallagher's book *Teaching Adolescent Writers* (2006) also includes a useful appendix with twenty-five prompts for timed writing.

Another type of high-stakes test we can help students with is the college application essay. Although these essays are not timed, they are often a required part of the college admission process and are high stakes for senior students. One can easily find lots of sample college application essay prompts online: ThoughtCo. (www.thoughtco.com) and the Princeton Review (www.princetonreview.com) are two sites where one can access lots of sample prompts, as well as other useful strategies and suggestions for writing the college application essay.

In *Teaching Adolescent Writing*, Gallagher (2006) notes that many skills needed to perform well on a timed writing task differ from those that students are taught for a multidraft essay. He presents a process for helping students understand and analyze the writing task called the ABCDs:

- Attack the prompt.
- Brainstorm possible answers.
- Choose the order of your response.
- Detect errors before turning the draft in.

Attacking the prompt involves circling words that indicate what to do: Draw an arrow from the circles to what the prompt specifically tells you to do, and number or order the circled words. Brainstorming includes generating ideas for possible answers and content by creating a quick list, map, web, chart, or other form of prewriting. The third step is choosing the order, essentially creating an outline for what the writer will do in each part of the essay. The final step is to detect errors before finishing, which includes taking the last few minutes to reread the essay and proofread (Gallagher, 2006).

Figure 8.1 shows two of Gallagher's students' use of the ABCD strategy for their on-demand essays. Notice how students have carefully attacked the prompt, completed a short brainstorming, and completed a quick scratch outline.

In attacking the prompt for a timed writing task, it is important to help students understand some of the academic language in the prompt, particularly the verbs, that may specify which type of essay they

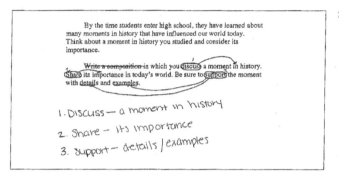

**Figure 2.5** *Attack the prompt*

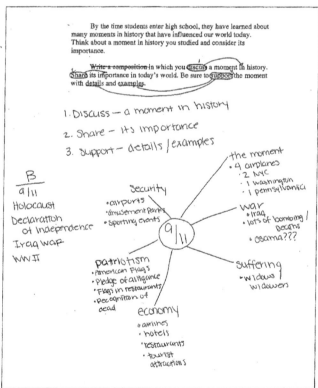

**Figure 2.6** *Brainstorm—9/11 with specific examples for each importance*

**Figure 8.1.   Attack the prompt/brainstorm. From *Teaching Adolescent Writers* by Kelly Gallagher, reproduced with permission of Stenhouse Publishers**

are to write and what they are expected to do. If you have taught students strategies for writing in different modes, then they will easily be able to recognize whether they are being asked to explain something, describe something, tell a story, or state opinions and make an argument.

Some of the verbs commonly used in standardized writing prompts include: *analyze, compare and contrast, critique, define, describe, discuss, evaluate, explain, identify, illustrate, interpret, justify, outline, respond, summarize, support,* and *synthesize.* Spend some time talking with students about the meaning of these words and making sure they understand how to approach the different types of writing they may be faced with.

The last step in Gallagher's ABCD method is particularly important to emphasize. Students often do not monitor their time very carefully during timed writing. They often use *all* of their remaining time for completing their response and do not save enough time at the end to reread what they have written. Stress the importance of saving the last few minutes of the allotted time to reread, quickly revise, and carefully edit the response for errors, such as in spelling, mechanics, sentence structure, grammar, and punctuation.

The AVID (Advancement via Individual Determination) program's *Write Path English Language Arts Teacher Guide,* developed by Hilary Crain, Michelle Mullen, and Mary Catherine Swanson (2002), includes useful advice for setting up and introducing timed writing in the classroom. They recommend the following steps:

1. Start with a good prompt for which students will be likely to generate good ideas.
2. Explain why timed writing is a skill students need to master and the importance of thinking and writing under pressure.
3. Place a start time and end time on the board.
4. Have students practice reading the prompt and underlining key ideas and instructions.
5. Review common essay format and such elements as a good introduction, several body paragraphs, and a conclusion.
6. Tell students to take about one-quarter of the total writing time to plan, by using a prewriting strategy like brainstorming, diagramming, clustering, mapping, and so on.

7. Explain to students that, in timed writing situations, it is OK to make mistakes, scratch out sections, erase lines, use arrows, and so forth. Have students focus on correcting obvious mistakes rather than worrying about neatness and appearance.

One positive thing is that more and more standardized writing tests and timed writing prompts are now being administered online, which allows students the benefit of using word-processing features, often including spell check and grammar check, although in some cases these features may be turned off.

If we are committed to spending some time teaching students how to approach timed and on-demand writing and having them complete practice timed writing in the classroom, then we are also faced with the need to score or evaluate these papers in order to provide feedback for students. Here are some suggestions for scoring of on-demand and timed writing tasks:

- Use the actual scoring rubric that will be used for the writing test. For example, if you have students write sample SAT essays, use the SAT scoring form. Scoring guides or rubrics for AP tests and IB tests may also be available. If students are practicing for a state writing assessment, then use your state's scoring guide for writing. These scoring guides often score the writing in four to six traits, such as ideas and content, organization, voice, word choice, fluency, and conventions. Some may also include citing sources as an additional trait.
- Create or use your own rubric or checklist to evaluate and provide feedback.
- Have students work with partners or small groups to score each other's essays using a rubric or checklist. They can also add some discussion or written commentary to make suggestions for their peers.
- Tell students ahead of time what you are specifically looking for in their response. Grade the papers only for specific criteria, such as content, number of paragraphs, organization, their use of the ABCD method, conventions, and so forth.
- Score the papers holistically with a scoring system, such as 1 for very low, 2 for needs improvement, 3 for good, 4 for very strong

and above average, and 5 for exceptional. Keep in mind that this method, while it may be the easiest, also provides very little feedback to students in terms of helping them understand what they need to do to improve.

- Give students credit for having written a sufficiently long piece in the given time frame. Remember, much of the benefit will be in the writing practice that students get from the exercise. More frequent timed writing will also help students become more comfortable with the process.

## KEY IDEAS IN THIS CHAPTER

- Students in high school and college are regularly expected to complete timed and on-demand writing tasks; therefore, ELA teachers should help prepare them for these often-high-stakes writing tasks.
- To be successful in timed writing tasks, students need to understand the prompt, generate ideas, organize their writing, and be aware of how their writing will be evaluated or assessed.
- As Gardner (2008) recommends, we can help students carefully define the writing task, scaffold the process for them, and provide practice in writing under pressure. It is important for students to focus carefully on the task and what is expected of them.
- Models of on-demand writing and practice SAT tests are useful resources for teaching on-demand and timed writing.
- There are several good options available for scoring and assessing students' on-demand writing, such as using scoring guides or rubrics, selective scoring, or holistic scoring.

# 9

# USING MULTIMODAL TEXT AND TECHNOLOGY TO SUPPORT WRITING

This chapter focuses on some techniques and resources for helping students learn how to incorporate multimodal text features into their writing. It also discusses ways to employ various forms of technology effectively to help nurture students' writing skills.

The Common Core State Standards (CCSS) for writing include two standards that address the use of technology. For grades 9 and 10, writing standard 6 states that students will be able to "[u]se technology, including the internet, to produce, publish, and update individual or shared writing products, taking advantage of technology's capacity to link to other information and to display information flexibly and dynamically" (Council of Chief State School Officers & National Governors Association, 2010). Writing standard 8, which focuses on the use of technology for research writing, states that students should be able to "[g]ather relevant information from multiple authoritative print and digital sources, including using advanced searches effectively, assess the usefulness of each source in answering the research question, integrate information into the text effectively to maintain the flow of ideas, avoiding plagiarism and following a standard format for citation" (Council of Chief State School Officers & National Governors Association, 2010).

In addition to the writing standards, the CCSS standards for speaking and listening also address use of technology and multimodal text for effective collaboration and presentations. Speaking and listening standard 2 for grades 9 and 10 states that students must "[i]ntegrate multiple sources of information presented in diverse media or formats evaluating the credibility and accuracy of each source." Speaking and listening standard 5 states that students must "[m]ake strategic use of digital media (e.g. textual, graphical, audio, visual, and interactive elements) in presentations to enhance understanding of findings, reasoning, and evidence to add interest" (Council of Chief State School Officers & National Governors Association, 2010).

New sets of national and state standards now articulate goals for students to be able to effectively use technology. In addition, the prevalence of technology and communication through various digital forms in the workplace and in the real world make it necessary for schools to take responsibility for helping students build skills using a variety of forms of technology. Adams (2008) aptly notes, "This is an era in which educators must acknowledge and build on the practices and processes students now use. Schooling is no longer defined by 1950's schoolhouses looming over middle America. Today's students embrace a tech literacy that many teachers overlook, ignore, or fail to embrace as wholeheartedly as the students do" (p. 99).

Many technology tools now facilitate not only helping students with the process of writing, from generating ideas to drafting and revising, but also for sharing and publishing their writing. Many features of technology can benefit and enhance the writing process. Revision is an important part of the writing process, and technology can facilitate revision in many ways.

When using technology, students have the opportunity to work on their writing at any time or place that they have access to the necessary tools: "Instead of being an activity that happens in a specific time frame and classroom, students' writing moves with them through multiple storage locations and technologies. They might start writing in Microsoft Word on a school computer, continue their writing on paper or on their smartphone or tablet on the way home from school or while waiting for an appointment, and complete it on a laptop at home" (Ferdig, Rasinski, & Pytash, 2014, p. 66).

Technology can also be beneficial in the editing and proofreading stages, with grammar-check and spell-check programs as well as other autograding programs (discussed later). And of course, technology can facilitate collaboration and provide students with an authentic audience through online spaces.

Research conducted as early as 2003 measured students' writing ability before and after being introduced to and learning to use laptops for writing. The study showed a 22 percent increase in the number of students who met or exceeded the standards in writing for their particular grade after a period of time of using laptops (Holcomb, cited in Demski, 2012). It is probably most effective for teachers to begin incorporating technology into writing instruction in the context of a school or districtwide initiative rather than an individual effort, which can be quite daunting. Demski (2012) reports on several district technology-supported writing initiatives that have shown an impact on student achievement scores. For example, the Student Writing Achievement through Technology-Enhanced Collaboration (SWATTEC) initiative in the Saugus Union School District (CA) provided netbooks to students in order to support writing across the curriculum. The SWATTEC initiative also provided students with authentic audiences for their writing by allowing them to post content online, making writing more interesting and relevant for students. Students also learned how to use the netbooks to conduct research as well as incorporate photos, videos, and source citations. Data collected following the SWATTEC initiative showed that student writing scores improved 10 percent during the first partial year of the initiative and 23 percent the following year.

Littleton, Colorado, Public Schools also began an Inspired Writing Initiative throughout the district. This initiative involved extensive professional development for staff, introduced teachers to netbooks, taught them how to operate the Linux operating system and cloud-based tools, and conducted writing workshops with teachers. Teachers also learned how to have students engage in peer review through wikis (Demski, 2012).

Demski (2012) notes, "With web 2.0 and social media tools, wireless connectivity, open source word processing and presentation software, cloud-based collaborative writing tools, and web-based writing tools . . . both districts built initiatives that have brought English language arts and classrooms as a whole into the 21st century—and made a significant impact on student learning" (p. 23). In the absence of a school- or districtwide initiative, however, teachers can still experiment with and explore different forms of technology and make an attempt to incorporate various technology platforms into their teaching in ways that will benefit students' writing.

## MULTIMODAL TEXT

In the twenty-first century, students need to become familiar with and proficient at using writing and communication in multimodal forms. Multimodal text is most simply defined as text that blends traditional print with visual, audio, and graphic elements, such as video and film, graphic illustrations, and even performances and spoken word. Most simply, multimedia, or multimodal text, is any text that includes more than just words alone. It is also, in some contexts, known as convergent media or transmedia.

Today, it is easy for student writers to incorporate various media into writing assignments and presentations. In an article on digital mentor texts, Werderich, Manderino, and Godinez (2017) note that digital writing is becoming more common and continuing to evolve in schools and, further, that "writing in print-only form is insufficient in the digital age" (p. 538). They argue that writing instruction should incorporate both print and digital text and that "explicit writing instruction needs to include scaffolding the use of multimodal texts for digital writing" (p. 538).

Visual writing can contain such elements as color and images in order to contribute to the overall message, thus integrating visual, audio, and spatial elements. In their article, Werderich, Manderino, and Godinez (2017) offer an example of a digital memoir writing assignment in order to show the ways in which multimodal elements can enhance such writing tasks. For this type of assignment, they refer readers to the StoryCenter website (www.storycenter.org), which can be used to teach digital writing elements, such as adding narration, sound effects, and images.

In some contexts, multimodal communication is referred to as convergent media, which is essentially taking multimodal elements and incorporating them into some kind of storyline in an interactive way, often including virtual media, animation, and simulation. Essentially, convergent media is a fusion of various forms of media to create an entirely new medium.

One thing you will want to do prior to asking students to incorporate multimodal elements in their writing is determine how much students already know about working with and manipulating digital media. You will likely find that some students are highly proficient in various forms of multimodal text, while others know very little about it and may require additional instruction. You may then need to create some minilessons to provide scaffolding for the incorporation of multimodal text.

It is important to remember, however, that, while technology can provide us with all sorts of amazing features and fancy bells and whistles, everything still depends on good, solid writing. Bad writing, even with the most amazing technology in the world, will still result in a bad product. Our students still need to learn the basic skills of clear, coherent, correct writing.

If you have a classroom set of computers or devices or if you depend on a computer lab, you will want to determine the software computers are equipped with. For example, is software for video- and audio-editing programs available? Do computers have such presentation programs as PowerPoint? Is a digital camera available, and can media files be saved and stored on portable drives?

Multimedia may include words, images, audio, and hyperlinks. One can incorporate links for images, film clips, and sound to enhance traditional writing. It is becoming more and more common for college writing assignments and classes to require students to not only produce high-quality presentations but also incorporate multimodal elements into class papers and writing assignments. Bullock and Daly Goggin (2016) note that college students will very likely be expected to create multimedia text that includes print, oral, and electronic elements, as well as words, images, audio, video, and hyperlinks. We should provide our students with a head start by teaching them how to incorporate multimodal elements in middle and high school and even as early as elementary school.

Teaching digital media means that students need to develop a new understanding of writing: Writing becomes not just print on the page but also relies on appropriate and effective forms of digital media and multimodal elements to accomplish the purpose of the writing, whether it is to inform, describe, or persuade. It is also important to help young writers learn to choose visuals that are appropriate for the audience and purpose: "In your academic writing, especially, be careful that any visuals you use support your main points—and don't just serve to decorate the text. (Therefore, avoid clip art, which is primarily intended as decoration.)

Images should support what you say elsewhere with written words and add information that words alone can't provide as clearly or easily (Bullock & Daly Goggin, 2016, p. 608). Also, make sure that students understand that copyright laws do cover visual material, and although it is probably OK to use a visual or image once without permission (for educational purposes), they must still clearly cite the source of the material.

Photographs can be used effectively to support many different modes of writing. Google Images (https://images.google.com), the National Geographic (www.nationalgeographic.com), and Getty (www.gettyimages.com) are great sources for photographs. Flickr (www.flickr.com) and PhotoBucket (http://photobucket.com) are useful for photo sharing. The National Geographic website is also a great source for maps.

For writing in online contexts, video clips can be used effectively simply by copying the video's web address and using it as a hyperlink within your text. Some students may choose to create their own videos with a program like iMovie or Windows Movie Maker or even a video made with a cell phone camera. Other popular movie-making apps include Magisto (www.magisto.com), Animoto (https://animoto.com), and Splice (http://splice.gopro.com). These programs allow students to create custom videos with Android and Apple devices.

Another possibility for multimodal text is to incorporate charts, graphs, or tables into the piece of text. The most common types of graphs are line graphs and bar graphs. Pie charts and other visuals, such as diagrams or flowcharts, can easily be designed and incorporated. Students can also add audio, video, hyperlinks, podcasts, and music or other sound files. There are several tips for incorporating visual material that you will need to make sure students understand:

- The visual should not be placed at the very beginning or very end of the text. It should be inserted into the text and placed close to where the material is being discussed.
- In academic writing, visuals should always be labeled and numbered. Generally, the words *figure* and *table* are used, along with a number. For example, the first visual presented may be a bar graph labeled "Figure 1"; the second might be a pie chart labeled "Figure 2"; the third might be a diagram labeled "Figure 3"; and

the fourth might be a table, which should be labeled "Table 1." Along with the numbered label, students should include a title or caption for the visual. For example, "Figure 3: Diagram of a seatbelt locking mechanism."

- Students should not just insert visuals into their writing and expect readers to figure out what they mean. The writer should always refer the reader to the visual with signal phrases, such as "Figure 1 shows" or "Refer to Figure 2," and include a brief summary of what the visual shows.

- Students may want to edit multimodal material before incorporating it into the work. For example, Photoshop can be used to edit, crop, or enhance a photograph. Video, audio, and podcasts can also be shortened. Caution students, however, that the work should only be edited in a way that does not change the meaning or misrepresent the content. The edited version must still be true to the original in content and intent. Charts and graphs can also be edited in an unethical way; for example, by changing the scale on a bar graph to overemphasize or underemphasize the data (Bullock & Daly Goggin, 2016).

- Cite the source of all images that are not self-generated. This can be done with a simple parenthetical citation in the text and a full citation in the works-cited page, the same method used for all other source material in the document.

- Advise students that, if they are publishing the writing in online formats, they will need to have permission to reprint any copyrighted visual material. Any visuals or images taken from the internet are copyrighted, unless they specifically state the material is available for free. Creative Commons (https://creativecommons.org) provides visuals and materials with conditions for their use; licensed material is made available by the originators, and others can use the material as long as certain simple rules are followed. Google Images is another good way to find visuals and identify the conditions for their use. Simply open Google, click on the "Images" link, and search for an image. After selecting an image, click "Tools" at the top of the page, and then "Usage Rights." This link will specify whether the image is labeled for reuse, with or without modifications, and commercial or noncommercial use, with or without modifications.

White and Morsink (2014) use the term *malleable genre approach* to help students use various genres, styles, and conventions. With this approach, students "digitally augment, alter, or replace any number of elements of the assignment" (pp. 44–45). They encourage students to incorporate digital elements as long as they serve to make the piece of writing more effective. They note that this procedure encourages students to think more about their purpose and audience and engage in deeper thinking about the relationship between writing and communication.

The sample activity White and Morsink (2014) describe is a sixth-grade inquiry project, using Wonderopolis (http://wonderopolis.org), which is a collection of daily "wonders," short pieces of text organized around answering a question, such as "Why do mosquito bites itch?" or "What is a sonic boom?" Students were required to come up with a question of their own, do research online, study various textual models, and write their own "wonders," incorporating digital elements. Each student then became an expert on the particular topic.

Mills (2014) also describes his particular approach to "digital content curation," recommending it as a method to use multiple literacies. His method is also inquiry-based learning that encourages student collaboration and multimodal comprehension. Students need to start with a purpose and topic; then find and select content and useful materials; customize the digital content, which can include reformatting and editing; and share with others through social media or online forums. Mills (2014) describes his students curating their own collection of web-based materials using Padlet (https://padlet.com) and Blendspace (www.tes.com/lessons), which provide an easy way to add multimedia and customize layout in a way that is not text based.

Huff (2017) describes a project she used in conjunction with teaching American literature, in which students created their own digital narratives. They first studied numerous examples of digital storytelling, generated ideas for potential topics, wrote scripts for their video narratives, and then began gathering images and video clips to create their digital stories. The students then recorded voiceover for their videos using sound-editing software (GarageBand [www.apple.com/mac/garageband] and Audacity [www.audacityteam.org]). Huff (2017) notes that "many video editing programs are available and make digital storytelling production relatively easy and also ensure that all of our students have the same access to the tools" (p. 35). Finally, students used iMovie (www.apple.com/imovie) to arrange images and sound for their stories, incorporating music as well to create appropriate mood. In her evaluation of the digital narrative project, Huff (2017) notes that many students remarked that the digital story was their favorite project and that "digital storytelling can be adapted for a variety of curricular purposes while offering students an engaging and increasingly necessary way for communicating in the digital world. . . . It offers students another writing genre in which to work" (p. 37).

Another great resource for digital content worthy of mention is the Google Suite (https://gsuite.google.com), in addition to Google Images mentioned earlier. Google Slides (https://docs.google.com/presentation/u/0) has an option for creating a photo album or a portfolio. If you have traditionally had students keep a writing portfolio, you might consider using the Google portfolio option as an online alternative.

## GOOGLE CLASSROOM

Google Classroom (http://classroom.google.com) is a free online service for schools that anyone with a Google account can access. Google Classroom can benefit and facilitate teaching writing in several ways. Teachers can easily set up classes, invite their students, and then share information and documents with them. You can create assignments, send announcements, and communicate with students. Class materials are automatically saved in Google Drive folders.

Students working on writing projects, for example, can share materials in Google Classroom and collaborate with each other, and teachers can monitor who has and has not completed the work. The tool is very useful for providing students with direct, timely feedback on assignments and grades. Here are some Google Classroom features that are particularly useful for writing instruction:

- You can create an assignment, include a description of it, and also attach supporting documents and materials, including videos.
- It is an easy way to go paperless. Rather than passing out and collecting paper, you can create a blank Google Doc or a template

for students to use, as well as have students submit their final papers to the site.

- When students have finished a writing assignment, it can be placed easily into the teacher's Google Drive.
- You can facilitate collaboration and collaborative writing assignments or projects. You can create a document and give all students access to it, letting them edit and contribute to it.
- You can also provide feedback to students during the writing process rather than just when grading the completed assignments. You can access assignments as students are working on them and insert comments and feedback.
- If you have ever graded a set of essays by hand and found yourself writing the same comment over and over again, you will appreciate the fact that you can provide common notes for all students, as well as provide individual feedback.

If you would like to learn more about Google Classroom, you can go to Google Help (https://support.google.com). There is also a useful tutorial available at Educational Technology and Mobile Learning (www.educatorstechnology.com/2015/01/everything-teachers-need-to-know-about.html).

## WRITING IN ONLINE SPACES

Today, students are expected to be able to write for many different purposes, and many forms of writing will be digital. Technology has changed the modes for communicating as well as the writing process itself (Valentino Drew, 2014). Valentino Drew (2014) recommends that teachers set up digital spaces for students to collaborate in an online writing community. This involves creating a space and providing laptops or tablets for students to use.

Valentino Drew (2014) also recommends establishing principles and acceptable use guidelines for students. Students can then use digital resources to plan their writing, draft, revise, edit, and publish. The space created can be Google Docs or some other program that allows for document sharing, such as Blogger (www.blogger.com) or Edublogs (https://edublogs.org). The teacher can then create the assignment, provide minilessons, provide feedback to students throughout the process, and have students share and collaborate in their writing (Valentino Drew, 2014).

Campbell (2014) defines *online collaborative writing* as "writing between collaborators for the purpose of creating a new work, such as a report, manuscript, poem, rap, song, or even graphic organizer . . . . one piece of writing to which all the writers contribute their thoughts, words, and research at every stage of the writing process" (p. 125). There are numerous web-based and cloud applications that can be used to facilitate collaborative writing:

- Etherpad (http://etherpad.org)
- Google Drive (https://drive.google.com)
- Prezi (www.prezi.com)

In collaborative writing spaces, writing can take place synchronously or asynchronously. The sites also have comments and notes features that allow students to provide feedback for each other (Campbell, 2014).

Google Suite (also known as Google Drive or Google Docs), like other online document-sharing spaces, has many potential uses for facilitating the teaching of writing. Most simply, students can submit papers by sharing with the instructor. You can critique, make comments, and edit the submissions. Most students today are comfortable with using Google Docs, and many of them use Google Docs exclusively. They simply log into their accounts. You can have them create a folder and label it with their name and class period, and then share with the instructor. You can then go to your Google Drive and create a folder for each class. Scroll down to highlight student names, and then drag them to the appropriate class folder.

Inside students' folders, they can create a "grade me" folder. The teacher can then read, edit, comment, and grade the paper. You could also create a "rough draft" folder as well as a "final copy" folder. Simply right click and touch "Share" to share documents. It's easy to move folders by dragging and dropping them.

Google Docs is also very useful for shared and collaborative writing assignments. Have students go to the class folder and create documents or slides and share the document with the other students in the group and with the teacher, if you want to be able to monitor the group work.

You can also have them wait until they are ready to submit before sharing with you.

Another way that Google Docs can help students is during the pre-writing process. You can use Google Forms, not only to create quizzes, but also to create graphic organizers and templates for writing assignments. Go to "Forms," choose "Blank Form," and then design a document. Create a short URL by going to "https://goo.gl" and then share the URL with students. You can also upload audio, video, and print files to Google Forms (https://docs.google.com/forms/u/0).

Moonen (2015) describes how she used Google Docs to help ninth-grade students with their writing skills. She decided to use a collaborative writing process. Google Docs provided the platform for the group planning and writing and allowed students to work together in real time and discuss and comment on the essays as they developed. Moonen (2015) notes, "Google Docs software presents all of the obvious features of word-processing packing; its additional advantage is that documents can be viewed and simultaneously edited by as many people as have been given access" (p. 8).

Moonen's (2015) first step was to have one student in each group create a Google Doc and share it with the other group members and her. Each student was given particular areas of responsibility for the writing and was expected to provide feedback for others throughout. Their comments addressed the argument and use of evidence, as well as grammar and conventions. Moonen (2015) notes that the process produced more substantial essays, where students were challenged to incorporate more research and evidence. It also allowed her as the instructor to provide feedback to the group and evaluate each student's contribution.

It is easy for teachers to provide feedback for students by highlighting or using the "Comment" tab. Comments will show up on the right side of the screen. If students use their cell phones for class work, have them download the Google Drive app. Keep in mind that Google Suite continues to evolve, and you can expect frequent changes and updates to the service. Therefore, you may find that the information contained here may not be 100 percent accurate at any given time.

Another option for online writing spaces is wikis, web applications that facilitate collaboration and content modification. Wikis "allow different writers to insert written content as well as formatting and design features like images and graphics, audiovisual components, and hyperlinks on the page" (Salter Thornton, 2014, p. 141). They also provide easy ways to incorporate multimodal text.

Salter Thornton (2014) describes one particular four-step model for using wikis. First, students generate a topic that lies within the subject area or theme the teacher has selected. Students then begin researching and writing about the topic and synthesize the information on the wiki page. The next step is to work on another student's writing topic by elaborating on or expanding it.

Next, they work toward embellishing a third wiki page with videos, websites, blogs, articles, graphics images, pictures, music, and so forth. Finally, students return to their own pages, read through, note changes made by other students, and make their final edits, attending to matters like citing sources, conventions, and formatting and layout.

"Wikis in Plain English" (www.commoncraft.com/video/wikis) is an online video that provides an overview and more information about using wikis (Salter Thornton, 2014). Another useful online space is Voicethread (https://voicethread.com), which is a multimedia presentation tool. Students can write and upload images, documents, or videos. It also facilitates collaboration among students, allows for collaborative writing and presentations, and creates an authentic audience for students because students can publish their written products online. Stover and Young (2014) recommend that, before using Voicethread, you should review and become familiar with the website, perhaps even create your own to provide an example for students. Students may also need some instruction on how to capture digital images, upload them, and use the "Comment" feature. They also recommend using Voicethread for peer response and feedback and for enhancing the revision process, in general.

As mentioned, online writing spaces provide many opportunities for peer review. In the article "Peer Review in a Digital Space," Holmes and Reed (2014) recommend beginning by providing students with examples of good as well as poor peer reviews in order to help students conduct peer reviews that are analytical, challenging, and respectful of other students.

Students can work in writing groups within a digital space like Google Drive, Voicethread, WordPress (www.wordpress.com), Blogger, or Eli Review (https://elireview.com) in order to respond to content and style and ask questions. Holmes and Reed (2014) note that peer review improves students' writing and critical-thinking skills: "Because this work takes place in digital social environments, where pairs of students, small groups, and whole classes can collaborate, every student engaged in digital peer review can access every other student's work, peer reviews, and teacher comments" (p. 193). All of these sites mentioned here can be used for free.

## A SAMPLE MULTIMODAL PROJECT: PERSONAL CULTURE EXPLORATION PROJECT

This project was designed by English teacher Cara Fortey for her World Literature and Culture class. It illustrates the types of projects and activities that teachers can design to combine traditional written text with multimodal elements. The project involves students in an activity that helps them explore the concept of culture, while also exploring their own personal cultural backgrounds and completing a written assignment incorporating multimedia. The following is a description of the project.

—◦∿◦—

### Personal Culture Exploration Project

As part of our exploration of culture this year, each of you will research your own ethnic and cultural origins. There may be one or a combination of several. If you are one, please try to be as regionally specific as you can. (If you truly do not know your heritage, please talk to me individually.)

The project will culminate in a written project with an opportunity for an extra-credit presentation. Please let me know as soon as possible if you wish to do a presentation, as I will need to block time for it.

The project has six parts:

### I. Literature

Literature can be novels, plays, short stories, poems, or similar types of writing.

- Research and find a book (preferably a novel) from your personal culture. Read it. Write a short (two- to three-paragraph) synopsis and a slightly longer (three- to four-paragraph) review.
- Additionally, create an annotated list (a one-paragraph summary of every other work with the date of publication, author, and genre) of at least five works of a variety of genres and authors. These are, essentially, things you could have chosen to read but didn't. One poem should be presented in its entirety. Please choose works that you think are most representative of your culture.

## 2. Music

This includes popular and traditional music. Provide a list of artists and songs from your ethnicity(ies). You should have three to four songs, minimum, covering a significant span of time. For extra credit, you can provide a CD of several selections that are reasonable in length and representative of your culture. If you choose to do an oral report, these may be embedded in the presentation or be playing simultaneously.

## 3. Art

This covers both recent and historical art. Provide pictures of art from your culture—this can be sculpture, paintings, drawings, or other genres. Provide at least two pictures.

## 4. Icons

Highlight at least two historical, popular, or heroic figures from your culture—one more recent and one from a previous era. Provide brief biographical details about the people and what makes them important in your culture, as well as a picture of them.

## 5. Sources

Keep track of where you get your information, pictures, and music, and create a works-cited list at the end of your presentation. Please use MLA format.

## 6. Flag

Each person will create their own ethnic and cultural flag. This will *not* be a reproduction of a national flag. This will be a representation of what your culture and ethnicity mean to *you*. Fabric, sharpies, and art supplies will be provided, but designs can be drawn, sewn, glued, painted, or something else to express your own feelings about your origins. The design must be appropriately sized for the fabric and visible from a distance. Flags can be one- or two-sided. This project will be done in class.

———⊱✦⊰———

The Personal Culture Exploration Project obviously incorporates several different multimodal elements. Once Ms. Fortey had identified the elements she expected students to incorporate into the assignment, she needed to begin exploring various multimedia platforms and programs that would allow students to post and present their projects online and would also allow her to use the platform to grade the assignments. Ms. Fortey also needed to find multimedia programs that could potentially work for students to design a digital flag rather than create an actual physical flag (for the sixth element of the assignment). If students chose to design a physical flag, they could use photographs of it to incorporate into the final project and multimedia presentation.

Ms. Fortey came up with several options that she could share with her students. Ultimately, she decided to have them upload their final multimodal projects to Google Classroom. She was then able to use the "Grading" and "Comment" features of Google Classroom to evaluate the projects. However, she found that the grading features built into Google Classroom were not ideal for evaluating and commenting on students' work.

There are several possible options for students to use in designing their project. One option is Google Drive. There is a Google drawing app that can be found under the "New" menu. Select the "New" tab, and then scroll down to "More" and select "Google Drawings." Google Slides is another feature that provides some options for drawing and creating in multimedia formats. Other possibilities include Adobe Illustrator (www.adobe.com/illustrator), Adobe Dreamweaver (www.adobe.com/Dreamweaver), Adobe Creative Cloud (www.adobe.com/CreativeCloud), and Sketchpad (https://sketch.io/sketchpad). Students could also, of course, also design their own webpages or just use the drawing features of Windows.

Two other programs that provide many useful features, with lots of creative elements and flexibility, are unfortunately not free. Unless they were used quite extensively, they might not be worth the expense: Piktochart (www.piktochart.com) and Canva (www.canva.com). Another thing that students might explore is a YouTube video illustrating how to use YouTube's photo slideshow tool called "Automatic Slide Show Maker for YouTube" (https://www.youtube.com/watch?v=_6nq36sUhAo). There is also a website that illustrates the interactive elements of Google Drawings (http://ditchthattextbook.com/2015/09/24/google-drawings-interactive-posters-no-glue-sticks-necessary) and a description of a semi-interactive Google Slide show called a "slide book" (https://www.google.com/slides/about).

Figures 9.1 and 9.2 show two students' personal culture flags created for the last stage of the project. Unfortunately, the visuals do not show the students' use of color in their flags.

## EDITING AND GRADING PROGRAMS

Technology has made available many programs and features that make the grading load that all ELA teachers face somewhat more manageable. Just as students are using new platforms and technological tools to write and revise, their teachers should also consider making use of some of the available editing and grading programs that allow you to do the grading online rather than collecting stacks of hard-copy papers and essays.

A great resource for online grading is Turnitin (www.turnitin.com). Turnitin is a plagiarism checker, but it also provides a feedback studio, autograder program, and use of quick marks that can be easily inserted

**Figure 9.1.   Mayely's personal culture flag. Reprinted with permission**

into students' submitted papers. If your district or school has a subscription to this site, it is easy to set up classes, provide students with their class ID and password, and require them to submit their papers to the website. You can construct your own grading rubric for particular assignments or make use of a number of existing rubrics for various types of assignments. You can quickly mark a number of common errors and can add your own custom grading marks, make comments directly on

**Figure 9.2. Clara's personal culture flag. Reprinted with permission**

the papers, and make written or voice comments for students to review. If the autograder misinterprets or marks things that are not correct or do not apply, you can easily dismiss them. You can also verify that students have reviewed their graded papers and communicate with students by e-mail. The site also now has a peer-review component for students to provide feedback for other writers.

Automated essay scoring (AES) software can provide students and teachers with feedback and resources for revising and correcting errors.

Usually, these programs are made up of several different computer programs in one location that provide feedback during and after the writing process. They also provide more detailed responses than ordinary word-processing software, often comparing students' papers with a bank of anchor paper (Gollnitz, 2014). While many of us may be somewhat skeptical of automated grading programs, they may indeed provide some benefits for students (and teachers). For automated scoring programs, Gollnitz (2014) recommends Educational Testing Service (www.ets.org) and Vantage Learning (www.vantagelearning.com), although these resources involve a per-student fee.

Automated grading programs often involve the student copying and pasting their documents into a textbox, and then the program generates a report, identifying problems with language, grammar, and other conventions. Students may then be more aware of which areas of their writing they need to work on before completing their final copies. Some of these same types of online programs are available and linked to writing handbooks and ELA textbooks (such as Pearson or Holt, Rinehart, and Winston). Gollnitz (2014) observes that, with automated programs, "students can use all of the tools available to revise their writing. Feedback reports show writers how well they have performed, and the process of revising serves as a learning activity. Again, students make the decision about when to submit a final copy of their writing for teacher review."

Another option for evaluating and grading student writing is using digital writing portfolios. Students can use Google Docs or Google Slides to create and maintain digital portfolios. Some teachers choose to assign grades by evaluating the body of work in the portfolio at regular intervals. Some may assign students to write five essays and then review their portfolios to choose the two that the teacher will grade.

Whether portfolios are digital or hard copy, they serve the same purpose: "A portfolio of writing includes a writer's best work and, sometimes, preliminary and revised drafts of that work, along with a statement by the writer articulating why he or she considers it good" (Bullock & Daly Goggin, 2016, p. 318). Of course, the advantage of a digital portfolio is that it can also contain multimodal elements, and students have more choice of design features. Students should attempt to identify which design elements will be most appropriate and help guide readers through the content.

Bullock and Daly Goggin (2016) provide several types of items that you may or may not choose to have students include in their portfolios. While most traditionally include writing samples, final copies, and best pieces, you might also include the following:

- Freewriting, outlines, or other prewriting activities
- Drafts
- In-class writing assignments
- Source material
- Tests and quizzes
- Peer responses to drafts
- Conference notes, error logs, and other course materials
- Electronic and digital materials and graphics
- The writer's reflection on the work

The last bullet listed is one of the most important elements: the student self-assessment.

The reflection sgives students the opportunity to evaluate their own work critically, reflect on what they have learned, and set goals for themselves. The self-assessment might be in the form of a letter, or you may ask students to address specific questions. You may ask for students to evaluate each piece of writing, make an assessment of his or her writing overall, choose a best piece of writing, discuss overall growth as a writer, describe writing habits and processes, and analyze overall class performance (Bullock & Daly Goggin, 2016). Most teachers find that the self-assessment and reflection pieces of the portfolio are most valuable because too often students do not go back and look at their previous essays and papers for the purpose of assessing how their writing has changed and improved.

This chapter provides ideas and options for making use of various forms of technology to help adolescents improve their writing. It also provides starting points for incorporating multimodal elements into student writing. New forms of technology and innovative new tools are popping up every day, so in the future, you will no doubt have new options and resources at hand.

## KEY IDEAS IN THIS CHAPTER

- Common Core writing standards 6 and 8 address the use of technology in writing, and speaking and listening standards address use of technology and multimodal text for collaboration and presentation.
- Schools must take responsibility for helping students learn to effectively use technology to prepare them for the real world and future careers.
- Many features of technology can enhance and benefit the writing process and can facilitate revision.
- Some schools and school districts have undertaken initiatives to incorporate technology into writing instruction.
- Multimodal text blends traditional print with visual, audio, and graphic elements.
- Many students are highly proficient in using various forms of multimedia, while others require additional instruction.
- Images, photos, video, charts, graphs, tables, and hyperlinked material are all common forms of multimodal text.
- Students must be taught conventions for incorporating multimodal materials into traditional text.
- Google Classroom is an effective resource for both teachers and students and can benefit writing instruction in many ways.
- There are many good strategies and project ideas for writing in online spaces, such as Google Docs, wikis, and Voicethread.
- There are several useful tools that can facilitate editing and grading of writing, including Turnitin, automated essay scoring programs, and online writing portfolios.

# REFERENCES

Adams, D. C. (2008). Gaga for Google in the twenty-first century advanced placement language classroom. *The clearing house, 82*(2), 96–100.

Andrews, R. (2009). *The importance of argument in education.* London: Institute of Education, University of London.

Berry, G. (2014). *Literacy for learning: A handbook of content-area strategies for middle and high school teachers.* Lanham, MD: Rowman & Littlefield.

Brookhart, S. M. (2013). *How to create and use rubrics for formative assessment and grading.* Alexandria, VA: ASCD.

Brooks, M. (2007). Lesson 5, being there: Using specific detail in narration. In C. J. Dixon (Ed.), *Lesson plans for teaching writing.* Urbana, IL: NCTE.

Bullock, R., & Daly Goggin, M. (2016). *The Norton field guide to writing with readings* (4th ed.). New York: W. W. Norton.

Campbell, L. O. (2014). Using technology for collaborative writing. In R. E. Ferdig, T. V. Rasinski, & K. E. Pytash (Eds.), *Using technology to enhance writing: Innovative approaches to literacy instruction* (pp. 125–31). Bloomington, IN: Solution Tree.

Carnegie Mellon University. (2015). Why are students coming into college poorly prepared to write? *Eberly Center for Teaching Excellence and Educational Innovation, Carnegie Mellon University.* Retrieved from https://www.cmu.edu/teaching/designteach/teach/instructionalstrategies/writing/poorlyprepared.html.

Coleman, D., & Pimentel, S. (2012). Revised publishers' criteria for the Common Core State Standards in English language arts and literacy, grades 3–12. Retrieved from http://www.corestandards.org/assets/Publishers_Criteria_for_3-12.pdf.

Council of Chief State School Officers & National Governors Association. (2010). *Common Core State Standards for English language arts and literacy in history, social studies, science and technical subjects.* Retrieved from http://www.corestandards.org/wp-content/uploads/ELA_Standards1.pdf.

Crain, H., Mullen, M., & Swanson, M. C. (2002). *The write path: Teacher guide for English language arts.* San Diego, CA: AVID Program.

Demski, J. (2012). Building 21st century writers. *T H E journal, 39*(2), 23.

Ferdig, R. E., Rasinski, V., & Pytash, K. E. (Eds.). (2014). *Using technology to enhance writing: Innovative approaches to literacy instruction.* Bloomington, IN: Solution Tree.

Fleming, N. (2012, Sep. 14). NAEP shows most students lack writing proficiency. *Education week, 32*(4). Retrieved from https://www.edweek.org/ew/articles/2012/09/14/04naep.h32.html.

Fredricksen, J. E., Wilhelm, J. D., & Smith, M. W. (2012). *So what's the story? Teaching narrative to understand ourselves, others, and the world.* Portsmouth, NH: Heinemann.

Gallagher, K. (2006). *Teaching adolescent writers*. Portland, ME: Stenhouse.

Gallagher, K. (2011). *Write like this: Teaching real-world writing through modeling and mentor texts*. Portland, ME: Stenhouse.

Gardner, T. (2008). *Designing writing assignments*. Urbana, IL: NCTE.

Geye, S. (1997). *Minilessons for revision: How to teach writing skills, language, usage, grammar, and mechanics in the writing process*. Spring, TX: Absey.

Gollnitz, D. L. (2014). Automated essay scoring software. In R. E. Ferdig, T. V. Rasinski, & K. E. Pytash (Eds.), *Using technology to enhance writing: Innovative approaches to literacy instruction* (pp. 211–19). Bloomington, IN: Solution Tree.

Graham, S., & Perin, D. (2007). *Writing next: Effective strategies to improve writing of adolescents in middle and high schools: A report to the Carnegie Corporation of New York*. Washington, DC: Alliance for Excellent Education. Retrieved from www.all4ed.org/files/writingnext.pdf.

Holmes, L., & Reed, D. (2014). Peer review in a digital space. In R. E. Ferdig, T. V. Rasinski, & K. E. Pytash (Eds.), *Using technology to enhance writing: Innovative approaches to literacy instruction* (pp. 193–98). Bloomington, IN: Solution Tree.

Huff, D. (2017). Telling the story of America: Digital storytelling projects in American literature. *English journal, 106*(3), 32–37.

Johnson, L. L., & Sieben, N. (2016). Reframing readiness: Minding the gap, reframing writing as creative problem solving. *English journal, 106*(1), 80–83.

Kiester, J. B. (2006). *Blowing away the state writing assessment test: Four steps to better writing scores for student of all levels* (3rd. ed.). Gainesville, FL: Maupin House.

Kohn, A. (2006). Speaking my mind: The trouble with rubrics. *English journal, 95*(4), 12–15.

Lannon, J. M., & Gurak, L. T. (2011). *Technical communication* (12th ed.). Boston: Longman/Pearson.

Mabry, L. (1999). Writing to the rubric: Lingering effects of traditional standardized testing on direct writing assessment. *Phi delta kappan, 80*(9), 673.

Macrorie, K. (1998). *The I-Search paper: Revised edition of searching writing*. Portsmouth, NH: Heinemann.

Mills, M. S. (2014). Digital content creation. In R. E. Ferdig, T. V. Rasinski, & K. E. Pytash (Eds.), *Using technology to enhance writing: Innovative approaches to literacy instruction* (pp. 133–38). Bloomington, IN: Solution Tree.

Moonen, L. (2015). "Come on guys, what are we really trying to say here?" Using Google Docs to develop year 9 pupils' essay-writing skills. *Teaching history, 161*, 8–14.

Nadell, J., Langan, J., & Comodromos, E. A. (2009). *The Longman reader* (9th ed.). New York: Longman/Pearson.

Reutzel, D. K., & Cooter, R. (2015). *Teaching children to read: The teacher makes the difference* (7th ed.). New York: Pearson.

Saddler, B., & Andrade, H. (2004). The writing rubric. *Educational leadership, 62*(2), 48–52.

Salazar, R. (2012, May 10). If you teach or write 5-paragraph essays, stop it! *Chicago now*. Retrieved from http://www.chicagonow.com/white-rhino/2012/05/if-you-teach-or-write-5-paragraph-essays-stop-it.

Salter Thornton, J. (2014). The 4E wiki model. In R. E. Ferdig, T. V. Rasinski, & K. E. Pytash (Eds.), *Using technology to enhance writing: Innovative approaches to literacy instruction* (pp. 141–48). Bloomington, IN: Solution Tree.

Seyler, D. U. (2012). *Read, reason, write: An argument text and reader* (10th ed.). New York: McGraw-Hill.

Spandel, V. (2006). Speaking my mind: In defense of rubrics. *English journal, 96*(1), 19–22.

Stover, K., & Young, C. (2014). Using 21st century technology to edit and revise. In R. E. Ferdig, T. V. Rasinski, & K. E. Pytash (Eds.), *Using technology to enhance writing: Innovative approaches to literacy instruction* (pp. 185–90). Bloomington, IN: Solution Tree.

Valentino Drew, S. (2014). Digital writing workshop. In R. E. Ferdig, T. V. Rasinski, & K. E. Pytash (Eds.), *Using technology to enhance writing: Innovative approaches to literacy instruction* (pp. 87–93). Bloomington, IN: Solution Tree.

Werderich, D. E., Manderino, M., & Godinez, G. (2017). Leveraging digital mentor texts to write like a digital writer. *Journal of adolescent and adult literacy, 60*(5), 537–46. doi:10.1002/jaal.584.

White, A., & Morsink, P. (2014). Fostering deep engagement with malleable digital genres. In R. E. Ferdig, T. V. Rasinski, & K. E. Pytash (Eds.), *Using technology to enhance writing: Innovative approaches to literacy instruction* (pp. 41–47). Bloomington, IN: Solution Tree.

Writing study group of the NCTE executive committee (2004, Nov.). NCTE beliefs about the teaching of writing. Retrieved from www.ncte.org/positions/statements/writingbeliefs.

Zinsser, W. (2001). *On writing well: The classic guide to writing nonfiction, 25th anniversary edition.* New York: HarperCollins.

# INDEX

# ABOUT THE AUTHOR

**Gregory Berry** teaches English at South Salem High School, where he has also been a teacher leader, instructional coach, and department coordinator, and is also an adjunct English instructor at Chemeketa Community College. He received his BA in English, BS in education, and MS in education from Eastern Oregon University and his doctorate in educational leadership, curriculum, and instruction from Portland State University in 2009. He is the author of *Literacy for Learning: A Handbook of Content Area Strategies for Middle and High School Teachers*, published by Rowman & Littlefield in 2014, and *Cultivating Adolescent Literacy: Standards, Strategies and Performance Tasks for Reading and Writing*, published in 2017.

Lightning Source UK Ltd.
Milton Keynes UK
UKHW01f0611260818
327810UK00001B/26/P

9 781475 841664